D1566317

ELECTING JESSE VENTURA

ELECTING JESSE VENTURA

A Third-Party Success Story

JACOB LENTZ

LYNNE
RIENNER
PUBLISHERS

BOULDER
LONDON

Published in the United States of America in 2002 by
Lynne Rienner Publishers, Inc.
1800 30th Street, Boulder, Colorado 80301
www.rienner.com

and in the United Kingdom by
Lynne Rienner Publishers, Inc.
3 Henrietta Street, Covent Garden, London WC2E 8LU

Library of Congress Cataloging-in-Publication Data
Lentz, Jacob, 1978–
    Electing Jesse Ventura : a third-party success story / by Jacob Lentz.
        p. cm.
    Includes bibliographical references and index.
    ISBN 1-58826-007-0 (alk. paper)
    ISBN 1-58826-031-3 (pbk. : alk. paper)
        1. Ventura, Jesse. 2. Governors—Minnesota—Election—Case studies.
3. Political campaigns—Minnesota—Case studies. 4. Third parties (United States
politics). I. Title.
JK6193 2001
324.9776'053—dc21   2001031626

British Cataloguing in Publication Data
A Cataloguing in Publication record for this book
is available from the British Library.

Printed and bound in the United States of America

The paper used in this publication meets the requirements
♾ of the American National Standard for Permanence of
Paper for Printed Library Materials Z39.48-1984.

5 4 3 2 1

To the decent, hardworking people of Minnesota,
who always make it nice to be home

And also to my father

CONTENTS

FOREWORD

SIDNEY VERBA

Few elections to a governorship in U.S. history have received as much attention as that of Jesse Ventura's 1998 victory in Minnesota. It was not only that Minnesota has always been a "special" state—a model state with a reputation for politics at a high level of civic virtue. Nor was it only that Ventura's election came at a time of turmoil and uncertainty in U.S. politics. Nor was it only that Jesse Ventura was an independent candidate running against both political parties. Nor was it just that he was a candidate with an unusual career background. It was all of these.

Few candidates have challenged the political establishment in such a striking manner. Ventura's was a victory that needed a close analysis. Jacob Lentz provides it. He gives a clear and thorough narrative of the election: where Ventura came from, how the primaries evolved, how the election was conducted. He has interviewed all the main participants. We hear the story from many perspectives, and from the inside. The narrative tells us a lot about Ventura's appeal. A third-party candidate has to overcome the wasted-vote logic: Why vote for someone who cannot win? Ventura turned it around: The other candidates have little to say, he seemed to argue; that's a real wasted vote.

Lentz's biggest contribution is not the narrative, however, but the analysis. He not only tells us the story of the campaign, but he explains why it came out the way it did. He looks closely at special features of election laws in Minnesota. He considers the voters and how they behaved—using some careful and sophisticated statistical techniques to tease out their motivation. And he looks at the role of the media.

Jesse Ventura's victory surprised and puzzled many. After reading this book, they may remain surprised—but a lot of the puzzle will be cleared up.

Sidney Verba
Professor of Government
Harvard University

ACKNOWLEDGMENTS

I owe debts of gratitude and in some cases large amounts of money to many people. First and foremost, Andrea Campbell at Harvard University deserves my thanks, for reasons too extensive to mention. Special thanks go to Alvin Tillery (who is now at Notre Dame, but whom I knew from Tufts), who was helpful and generous and patient during this project and in most of my other pseudo-academic endeavors. Thank you, also, to Sidney Verba for being so nice about this book.

I am grateful to Meg Marshall and Jim von der Heydt for reading pretty much the whole manuscript, for letting me bother them, and for helping me with a speech I had to write. Thanks to Anthony Loscalzo, Wheeler Thackston, Gene McAfee, Devesh Kapur, James Fowler, and generally anyone I may have taken a class from while a student in college. Thanks to Mike Cavanaugh, Bruce Watson, the Rudaleviges, and Tracy Marshall for chatting; to Becky for help with research; to SCH; to DC for the music, KCE for just being there, and DAK for staying up; and to EAP, JYY, MRH, RKK, AO, EJK, DOM, MJTM, DES, JEE, PTM, CAD, NCM, MNS, MCW, TEC '90, MMW, WBD, and, of course, SMJ-G. I also thank Dave, Paul (whoa), Joe, John, Pete, George, Kevin, Matt, Ken, Cabral, Vic, Shawn, Jessie, Kara, Sarah, Michelle, Chris, Emily, Tim, Sarah, Laura, and Ursula. I appreciate Jake Ewart and Tim Arnold for agreeing to the social euthanasia that is living with me. And Tom Wolfe, DFW, and the Boss, for getting me through the long nights. Anyone I forgot, thank you as well.

Special thanks to the people who cooperated and agreed to be interviewed for this project, all of whom had better things to do with their time, who were very patient, and who were all credits to their parties and their state. I would like to especially thank Dave Nimmer for his help, and also Bob von Sternberg for being so friendly and patient with me. A special thanks to Chris Georgacas, who was far more helpful than he had to be even if you include Minnesota Nice in your Composite Friendliness Index.

Finally, I would like to extend a special thank-you to the people who serve Minnesota in public office. In the course of this project I had the opportunity to speak with a host of Minnesota's leaders, including Arne Carlson, Mike Freeman, Skip Humphrey, Ted Mondale, and Jesse Ventura, as well as a host of party activists and government workers who work behind the scenes. I found them all, without exception and regardless of party, to be honest, dedicated, and genuinely concerned with doing good for the people of Minnesota. Except for Todd Boulevard of the Minnesota Monkey Party. That guy only cares about monkeys.

Jacob Lentz

I

INTRODUCTION:
THE SIGNIFICANCE OF MINNESOTA

A t first Jesse Ventura hesitated to declare victory. It was nearing midnight on the day of the election, and no winner had yet been declared in what had become a three-way race for governor. The crowd that had turned out for his election-night party was getting raucous (in a mosh pit), and as the Reform Party candidate waited backstage to address them, a local television station called the race and pronounced him victorious. But Ventura was skeptical—he did not understand how they could call the race with only 60 percent of the official vote counted. Not wanting to humiliate himself and his party by mistakenly declaring victory, he decided to tell the crowd only that whatever happened, he had at least been leading the vote count for a time. His supporters carried on their carousing while Jesse waited in another room. Only after the ABC and NBC affiliates called the race and state troopers arrived to protect the governor-elect did the reality of the win sink in. Maria Shriver called Ventura's wife on her cellular phone to congratulate them and arrange a live interview. Finally Ventura joined the party again, taking a seat in front of an enormous green-and-black banner as the crowd chanted, "Jes-se! Jes-se! Jes-se!" Once his supporters quieted down enough for him to talk, he voiced one of the most insightful sentiments of his public life: "We shocked the world!"[1]

The rise of Governor Jesse Ventura is one of the most surprising events to occur in the modern era of American politics. This book is an examination of the 1998 Minnesota gubernatorial election from the standpoint of political science. It has been admittedly easy to ignore the real implications of this election. After all, the governor is a man who invented his own name for its theatrical flair (his given name was James Janos) and whose fame originated in feigning athletic contests; he is a

I

hulking slice of humanity (well over six feet and thickly muscled) with a polished pate, twinkling blue eyes, and a gravelly yet oddly sonorous voice, who for no clear reason regularly dresses in military fatigues. It is probably not surprising, therefore, that much of the interest in Jesse Ventura flows from his entertainment value: A famous pro wrestler as governor of a state provides occasion to compare politics to cage wrestling and invent catch phrases such as "The Body Politic" and "body-slamming the system," all compounded by the fact that Ventura quickly revealed himself as unwilling to keep nearly anything floating through his head from leaving through his mouth. But that does not change the central question: What does it mean that Jesse Ventura won fair and square?

This book narrates the events of the campaign and election and wades through the commentary and punditry, the nonsense and bombast, to extract what can be had for real lessons. It is fair to say that there has been in the popular media and among the *cognoscenti* a large ratio of speculation on the proper interpretation of this election (it is surprisingly painful to listen to the endless torrent of self-assured political analysts proudly proclaiming the radical redefinition of politics with the importance of the "Ventura effect" and "Ventura voters") to actual attempts at intellectual understanding. It is my earnest hope that this book will be counted among the latter.

Chapter 2 is a narrative history of the election, from the days of nascent candidacies through the summer and the primaries, toward Ventura's emergence as a clear and legitimate alternative to the two major parties, to his final and eventual victory. This account of the race lays bare the inner workings of the individual campaigns, weaving numerous interviews with key participants and much heretofore unknown information into a coherent recital of events. Additionally, this story as it is here told confirms that campaigns do in fact matter (an issue of some debate), that the choices people make in real time can have the consequence of victory or defeat, and that macro events are not forged beyond the sovereignty of human action; this is not a vendetta of a desire to reconcile the idea of free will with a determined environment but, admittedly, it is still in keeping with the worldview of Henry Kissinger, who said, "As a professor, I tended to think of history as run by impersonal forces. But when you see it in practice, you see the difference personalities make."

Chapter 3 analyzes Ventura's victory. Who voted for him and why? Exit polling, official election statistics, and personal interviews are applied to various theories to test their relative value in explaining the election. Beyond who voted for Ventura (and conjectures about why they did), there is the question of how he won as the candidate of a third party. To examine this, several strings of data are interwoven to paint a picture of the perfect intersection of forces that when combined yielded a result opposite from what one generally expects from a third party.

Chapter 4 extracts from the election probable lessons for political science. These exist in three broad arenas of study. The first is the study of celebrity politics, which is not in itself surprising, of course; but it is surprising to see the ways in which Ventura's celebrity actually mattered—and didn't matter. Second, Ventura won the election by getting people who do not usually vote to come out and vote for him. That he did this in the specific context of Minnesota's unique electoral system begs reconsideration of how we answer the basic question "Why do people vote?" and thus voting theory is the second subject of this chapter. Third, Minnesota's election rules relative to those of other states, the polling taken throughout the race after specific events, and the failures of other third parties offer insight into the source and nature of the specific problems facing third parties in America. Moreover, by looking at other states' experiences with victorious third parties and comparing them to Minnesota, it is possible to sketch a new theory of third parties in America—one that foresees a possibility of their success.

This book is about political events in Minnesota in 1998. But it would be a poverty to take the these chapters in a vacuum, to try to understand the election as a thing unto itself, in ignorance of the larger context. If the end of a thing is its nature, then to begin to see what happened in Minnesota for what it is, one must start at the place in which it came to pass. Thus, in some regard this book and what it aims to accomplish cannot set forth without a knowledge of the people and their history.

Minnesota and the Meaning of History

"Lake Wobegon, where all the women are strong, all the men are good-looking, and all the children are above average . . . "
—Garrison Keillor

"Surely this is America's promised land."
— The Economist, July 1997[2]

That Minnesotans are different from other people is usually obvious to most visitors. Each of the fifty states has, to differing degrees, its own character, and some are especially distinctive in their styles and so are famously stereotyped. Minnesota stands out, though, because it tends to lie slightly below the Radar of Weird States. People know certain things about it—it is in the Midwest, the weather is very cold, the people have a funny accent, and many of them are big and blonde. It is also, many have heard, a nice place to live. But Minnesotans do not advertise themselves, partly because it's hard to be pompous about the things people notice, which is primarily that they are friendly, generally well educated, practical, and particularly earnest.

Those who study Minnesota's history are not particularly surprised to see consistent traces of a community-oriented, progressive ethic. Many observers link this tradition to the immigrant Scandinavians, more of whom settled in Minnesota than any other state in the Union, and who brought with them a sort of indigenous communitarianism.[3] Russell Fridley, former director of the Minnesota Historical Society, speaks of a "Minnesota Mystique" that he likewise ascribes to these nineteenth-century immigrants, an ethnic mix that remains pronounced and reinforced by the Germans (in the early 1900s, Scandinavians made up around 55 percent of the Minnesota population, Germans around 25 percent[4]). It can also be argued that Minnesotans are predisposed to cooperation not just because of their ethnicity but because of their weather. During the Minnesota winter, temperatures can stay in the minus double digits for weeks, and exposed flesh, even your eyeballs, can freeze in less than a minute, frostbite is part of growing up, and more people than you'd probably think have fallen through a frozen lake (often more than once). The incentive to cooperate is therefore pretty strong. But regardless of its source, communitarianism as a feature of life in Minnesota has been pronounced since its beginning, and it remains so in many ways today.

Because of the outward focus of life in the state and because Minnesota's most famous politicians—Hubert Humphrey and Walter Mondale—were Democrats, there is a popular impression that Minnesota is a liberal state. Minnesota's political culture, however, is more complicated than that. One writer accurately wrote that

> Image, culture, and lifestyle also belie the reputation of liberal Minnesota. Newcomers are often surprised by the state's essentially conservative personality. Minnesotans, it turns out, are frugal, disinclined to faddishness and outlandish behavior, taciturn, repelled by extravagance or waste, and leery of crazy new ideas. Liquor stores are closed on Sundays. Churches often are full on Sunday. The denizens tend to stare down their noses at you if you smoke, swear, talk loudly, wear bright colors or too much make-up.[5]

Minnesotans might be concerned with equalizing the common good and helping the less fortunate—and they are—but there exists in tandem a focus on self-control, individual initiative, and personal responsibility. Minnesota is, indeed, the epitome of what has been termed the moralistic political culture.

Fridley describes Minnesota's government as "a blend of frugality and limited government—but on top of that is the concern for community that pushes Minnesota toward orchestrated social welfare."[6] Arne Carlson, son of Swedish immigrants and governor for two terms until retiring in 1998, described Minnesota's way of approaching things this way: "A rather fascinating Scandinavian ethic that is sort of split. Very practical and hardworking on one hand, very liberal in other respects."[7] This mix has helped forge an especially high quality of life. A 1973 cover of *Time* featured a smiling Republican governor Wendell Anderson in his fishing boat and proclaimed "Minnesota: A State That Works." The piece said of the state, "If the American good life has anywhere survived in some intelligent equilibrium, it may be in Minnesota."[8]

For instance, it is a fact that the last bastion of corporate charity is the Minneapolis–St. Paul business community, where a gentlemen's agreement among seventy-eight Minnesota-based companies pledges 5 percent of earnings to charity, even as this sort of behavior has virtually died around the rest of the country.[9] This behavior led *Harper's* to write that "[the] archetypical man-who-has-made-it in, say, Miami may enjoy his leisure on a yacht, and in Hollywood among his collection of starlets—but if he lives in Minneapolis he would spend it in committees."[10]

The ethic that yields this behavior has caused the state to be one of firsts. Minnesota began in 1933 the first comprehensive program to assist students who otherwise could not afford college in getting a degree.[11] (Indeed perhaps the strongest Scandinavian contributions, as William Lass points out in his history of the state, is in the area of education; Norwegian and Swedish Lutherans were leaders in establishing educational institutions that have names like Augsburg, Gustavus Adolphus, and St. Olaf.)[12] The University of Minnesota began the nation's first vocational agriculture school in 1888.[13] The state saw some of the first children's libraries, and the bookmobile is a Minnesota invention as well, having made an appearance in St. Louis County in 1925.[14] The state legislature in 1876 created the nation's first forestry association, and the Minnesota State Park system is the largest in the country.[15] But Minnesotans are still wary of popular trends—it was only after most of the country had adopted state lotteries that the citizens here voted on and passed a state constitutional amendment to allow the legislature to operate a state lottery; soon thereafter, they passed another amendment to require that 40 percent of lottery proceeds be earmarked for an environmental trust fund.[16]

One can even look to something as seemingly tangential as public radio and find evidence of Minnesotans' sense of community obligation. The entire state is blanketed with NPR, brought from the Twin Cities to the hinterlands through twenty-four stations (there are more National Public Radio–member stations in this state than any other; California, twice as large and with several times the people, has only eleven).[17] Much more important, the way Minnesotans have perceived their duty to support it highlights their communitarian sensibility, as they contributed enough money to a Minnesota Public Radio (MPR) capital campaign that the station was able to completely overhaul its studios and equipment and remain one of the most solvent public radio affiliates in the nation. A statement by the president of the MPR in the official summary of the campaign as much as proclaims the unique Minnesota spirit in saying, "There are few communities where the value of public radio has been understood as well as it is here—and even fewer where public radio is considered a significant community institution that merits major philanthropic support."[18]

Minnesotans have worked together over time to create a high quality of life, and they have done a good job of it. The residents are among the most highly educated in the nation, with 31 percent of those over the age of 25 having college degrees, third only to Colorado and Maryland.[19] Minnesotans are by some measures the best-read people in the nation.[20] They have the longest life expectancy after Hawaii.[21] The school system is among the best in the nation; it is first in the rate of high school graduation.[22] It has the thirteenth highest standard of living in the United States, a rank that goes up significantly if one extends standard of living to incorporate the state's low crime rate and excellent health care.[23]

Civic engagement is likewise high. Almost 70 percent of Minnesotans attend religious services regularly, compared to just over 50 percent nationally.[24] Around 45 percent of Minnesotans attended community meetings in 1995 and over 49 percent volunteered their time, compared to 37 percent and 36 percent nationwide.[25] Voter turnout in the state during presidential elections has been consistently around 20 percent higher than the national average.[26] A recent study showed that Minnesota ranked fifth in overall turnout, behind Montana, South Dakota, Maine, and Wyoming.[27] In a 1995 Minneapolis *Star Tribune* poll, fully 75 percent of Minnesotans said that they were either "interested" or "very interested" in politics, and the same poll found that 16 percent of

Minnesota citizens had held political office, compared to 3 percent nationwide.[28]

Minnesotans like the way they do things in their state, and for good reason. As one observer pointed out, however, they "rarely feel that they are doing well enough in their politics and government. They invariably feel that they could be doing better. At times Minnesotans even seem to try to highlight their minor problems to be in tune with the rest of the nation, where the same problems are major."[29]

This is not the "famously liberal" state that stereotypes would have it be—this is a state whose people have always been conscious of a need to find ways to make things better but whose core worldview is in many regards a conservative one. The ability to embrace business while focusing on social welfare is the ethic that has made Minnesota unique, a place so confident in its ways and culture that it has historically desired to maintain a certain measure of isolation from the rest of the nation. By every measurement the quality of life there is extremely high. Minnesotans are, as a whole, dutiful, straightforward, and given to orderliness. But, as Jesse Ventura's election demonstrated, there is a major caveat.

Cantankerous Selves

"You are never, never to let the Vice Pres [Humphrey] attend any meeting on the legislative program. . . . I've never known anyone from Minnesota that could keep their mouth shut. It's just something in the water out there."
   —*President Johnson to domestic staffer Joe Califano*[30]

Historically, Minnesota has been as radical as it has been progressive. The duality of Minnesota's political temperament was expressed well by a writer who saw clearly these two sides of Minnesota's consciousness and wrote of "Minnesota's egalitarian progressivism, liberalism and tendency to want to fix every social problem; its moralistic and high-minded tone, steeped in Christian ideals and Utopian schemes; and a cussed independence, a populist impulse to overturn the establishment, and an unusual preference for third-party movements."[31]

Exactly one hundred years before electing a Reform Party governor, Minnesota elected its first third-party governor, John Lind, who was nominated by the Silver Republican Party but was also the nominee of the Populist and Democratic Parties under a unique tri-party arrangement

that gave the governorship to the Silver Republicans, the offices of lieutenant governor and attorney general to the Populists, and those of secretary of state and treasurer to the Democrats. This election, Russell Fridley claims, "opened a vein in Minnesota voters that would widen in the
early 20th century as they increasingly turned to third parties and became famous for casting split ballots."[32] (Lind's victory, like Ventura's,
was essentially a personal victory and not party-wide, "attributable primarily to [his] personal qualities and Scandinavian background.")[33]

When in 1912 Minnesota gave its electoral votes to Bull Moose
leader Teddy Roosevelt, Progressive candidates swept the state legislature as well.[34] In 1912 a nonpartisan law was enacted that banned political parties as a factor for municipal, county, and state legislative offices. A Socialist was elected mayor of Minneapolis in 1916.[35] For a
long time after the re-creation of Russia as the Soviet Union, high
school graduations in rural parts of Minnesota had students receiving
their diplomas file past both the U.S. and Soviet flags.

In 1915 a man named Arthur Townsley, a Minnesota school teacher
turned North Dakota farmer, formed the quasi-socialist Non-Partisan
League in North Dakota to represent farm interests. In 1917 the league
moved its national headquarters to St. Paul, and its membership rose
quickly. The league's leaders quickly realized that Minnesota's dual
agricultural and industrial bases could be tapped for their goals, and the
Republicans so dwarfed the Democratic Party in Minnesota that the latter essentially could not be counted as a major party, and the league realized that it had an opportunity. Thus was born the Farmer-Labor Party
in Minnesota. The party first appeared on the ballot in 1918 and was
consciously class based, full of avowed socialists in its highest ranks
and deploying vaguely communist rhetoric in its platforms (the party's
1934 platform called for a "cooperative commonwealth" in the state and
the nation).[36]

The Non-Partisan League challenged Republican governor Joseph
Burnquist in 1918 with a candidate by the name of David Evans. Told
by the attorney general that he needed a party label, he and other league
members settled on Farmer-Labor Party.[37] Evans finished well ahead of
the Democrat in the race, thus turning the Farmer-Labor Party into one
of the state's major parties literally overnight. In 1923 the Farmer-Laborites gained control of both U.S. Senate seats with the victory of
Magnus Johnson in a special election against Republican governor
Jacob Preus, a fierce antisocialist, for the seat of recently departed Senator Knute Nelson. Here was a character not unlike Ventura years later:
Johnson was castigated by his enemies as an unintelligent and ignorant

"dirt farmer." In response he entertained farm audiences by standing in a pile of manure and declaring that he was for the first time standing on a Republican platform.[38]

Perhaps the most famous Minnesota radical is Governor Floyd B. Olson, elected in 1930. Like Ventura, he grew up in a poor neighborhood in Minneapolis, which cultivated a sympathy with the disadvantaged. He put himself through law school at the University of Minnesota and was soon Hennepin County (Minneapolis) Attorney, a capacity in which he became known as a crusader against corruption and often, according to Russell Fridley, played up the extent of corruption for his own political advantage.

He lost the governor's race in 1924 as a Farmer-Laborite, but in 1930, after the stock market crash, he became the first Farmer-Labor governor in the state. Again, like Ventura, he tended to be greatly loved or greatly hated. He spoke Swedish, Norwegian, and Yiddish, which aided the effectiveness of his fiery oratory. He was widely seen as a potential vice president and even as potential presidential timber, and some saw his populism as a threat to the national Democratic Party. He once said, "I enjoy working on a common basis with liberals . . . , but I am not a liberal. I am what I want to be—I am a radical."[39] His political career was halted when he died of cancer in 1936, cementing his stature in the minds of Minnesotans for generations to come (something of which they are reminded each time they drive the Olson Memorial Highway in Minneapolis).[40]

Olson's years as governor were ones of massive social legislation. In 1933 a special set of "mortgage moratorium acts" was adopted to prevent foreclosures on mortgages, saving many of the state's farmers from bankruptcy.[41] In 1935 the state income tax was passed, and it was soon imitated around the country because of its progressive fairness. The income tax was responsible for saving the public schools in the state, which had been on the verge of collapse.[42] Olson also pushed through laws banning anti-union contracts and antistrike injunctions.[43]

In 1944, the Democrat and Farmer-Labor Parties merged into the Minnesota Democratic Farmer-Labor (DFL) Party.[44] It was in 1948, only four years after he helped found the state party, that Minneapolis mayor Hubert Humphrey's speech on civil rights drove the Dixiecrats from the Democratic Party.[45]

Since the formation of the DFL Party, the configuration of the political parties in Minnesota has tended to parallel national trends. One exception was the state's widely hostile reaction to McCarthyism. And after Watergate, the state Republican Party, in an effort to disassociate from the national party, adopted the label Independent Republican. It took until 1995 before the party decided to restore the earlier name.[46]

If it can be encapsulated simply, the Minnesota mind-set can be said to despise nonegalitarianism, hate dishonesty, and tear down people who put on airs. For instance, it has always been acceptable for wealthy Minnesotans—the McKnights, the Daytons, the Pillsburys—to build and live in expensive homes, but it was considered poor taste to let them be seen from the road. The families were loath to be seen as flaunting their wealth before the less fortunate, and as a general rule they have avoided even the appearance of doing so.[47]

David Nimmer, a well-respected former newspaperman and local journalism professor, speaks of "a certain kind of prairie populism" that distrusts the rich, the powerful, and those who show off.[48] The political manifestations of this sentiment are at times severe. When Walter Mondale resigned his Senate seat to assume the vice presidency, DFL governor Wendell Anderson resigned and his successor, lieutenant governor Rudy Perpich, appointed him to the Senate.[49] In the election of 1978, both Senate seats were open because of Hubert Humphrey's death early that year (his widow, Muriel, had been appointed by Perpich to serve out his term and was not seeking reelection). That year, in what is known as the Minnesota Massacre, the voters of Minnesota retaliated against the perceived underhanded deal-making between Perpich and Anderson, replacing both Senate seats with Republicans Rudy Boschwitz and Dave Durenberger and Governor Perpich with Republican Al Quie.[50]

When Senator Durenberger was accused of charging the government rent for a Minneapolis condominium by using his office allowance and calling his apartment his "local office," Minnesotans immediately dismissed him as even an option for reelection—the main debate in the state was not whether he should be forgiven but whether he should be allowed to finish his term before being replaced.[51] In 1992 the *St. Paul Pioneer Press* ran a series entitled "Bankrolling the Legislature" that created such a reaction among citizens that the state legislature passed a series of lobbying reforms in 1993 and 1994 that eventually banned gifts of any kind from lobbyist to legislator.[52]

In his 1951 essay "Prelude to Populism," Donald F. Warner wrote, "Through most of its history Minnesota has shown symptoms of political schizophrenia."[53] Consider U.S. Senators Paul Wellstone, known as "the most liberal man in the Senate," and Rod Grams, who has established himself as one of its most conservative members. In 1994, the American Conservative Union gave Grams a score of 100 (on a scale of zero to 100) and Wellstone a score of 4; the Americans for Democratic Action, using the same scale, gave Wellstone a score of 100 and Grams zero.[54] The thread between these two very different men, some say, is their essentially populist nature combined with a straight-talking honesty; both have championed unpopular causes. Mary McEvoy, a DFL executive, describes the Minnesota way of choosing leaders as putting a priority on honesty and humility:

> Like with Wellstone, the one thing we hear about him all the time is that people admire him, even if they disagree with him on everything. Or Rudy Boschwitz [who had made his money in the plywood business], when he was running for Senate in his plaid shirts, people had bought their plywood from this guy.[55]

Perhaps for these reasons, Ross Perot received 24 percent of the vote in Minnesota in 1992.[56] These antiestablishment, populist strains were a major theme of William Lass's history of Minnesota; a few years before the election of Jesse Ventura, he wrote, "Perhaps the most enduring trait of Minnesota's politics has been a certain maverick tradition. Minnesotans have been willing to experiment and to pioneer new political movements."[57]

The Minnesotan Way

The connecting thread of the two sides of Minnesota's civic sociology is egalitarianism—everything should be and is about the common good, and if that at times translates into populism, so be it (for instance, should Minnesota's being the first state to produce antismoking and educational choice bills[58] be seen as manifestation of the state's communitarian ethic or its radicalism?). Added to this is a willingness to try new things, to be unsatisfied with the status quo. There has always been a desire to change the way things are in attempting to improve them. Even the cut-and-dried *Economist* conceded that Minnesota's success is bound up in its culture, assigning partial credit to Minnesotans being "honest and hard-working" and "innovative."[59]

    Culture-focused historians and political economists—Daniel Elazar most famously[60]—have focused on Minnesota as the quintessence of a "moralistic" political culture—marked by positive, active government and citizen involvement. Minnesota's culture is distinct—a natural dichotomy of well-ordered communitarianism and radical populism. Although Minnesota's culture might make Jesse Ventura a less surprising governor, the state's mores are not the right explanation of his victory. His election had far more to do with the state's unusual institutions and rules. Despite the national media's apparent surprise, the election of an outspoken, charismatic, melodramatic populist in the state of Minnesota is not all that shocking.

Cultural explanations deserve skepticism, especially when they begin to place cultures up against each other and declare one superior. Minnesota is not perfect—I do not mean to suggest that it is—and indeed some have suggested that because the state has until recently remained relatively homogenous with so few social problems, it may in fact deal poorly with things that other states have been facing for years; moreover, it is fair to say that Minnesota's minority communities have not had an equal share of the benefits of Minnesota's egalitarian spirit. But that is not the concern of this book, and we can now begin to examine the decision made by the unique people of a unique state.

Notes

1. Bill Hillsman, CEO of North Woods Advertising and Ventura campaign political and media consultant, 26 August 1999, interview by the author, Minneapolis, MN.

2. "The Land of Good Lessons," *The Economist* 344 (5 July 1997), p. 28.

3. Webb Garrison, *A Treasury of Minnesota Tales* (Nashville: Rutledge Hill Press, 1998), p. 196.

4. Russell Fridley, former director of the Minnesota Historical Society, 2 August 1999, phone interview by the author, St. Paul, MN.

5. Dane Smith, "The 'L' Word," Minneapolis *Star Tribune*, 18 November 1994, p. 22A.

6. Russell Fridley interview, 2 August 1999.

7. Arne Carlson, 9 September 1999, interview by the author, Minneapolis, MN.

8. "Minnesota: A State That Works," *Time* 103, 7 (13 August 1973), p. 24.

9. "The Land of Good Lessons," p. 28.

10. John Fisher, "The Minnesota Experiment: How to Make a Big City Fit to Live In," *Harper's Magazine*, April 1969, p. 20, quoted in Daniel J. Elazar, Virginia Gray, and Wyman Spano, *Minnesota Politics and Government* (Lincoln: University of Nebraska Press, 1999), p. 16.

11. Garrison, *A Treasury of Minnesota Tales,* pp. 192–195.

12. Willam E. Lass, *Minnesota: A History* (New York: W. W. Norton and Company, 1998), p. 192.

13. Garrison, *A Treasury of Minnesota Tales,* p. 191.

14. Ibid., pp. 192–195.

15. Ibid., p. 190.

16. State of Minnesota, Secretary of State, Election Division, *Minnesota Legislative Manual, 1995–1996* (St. Paul: Offices of the Election Division, Secretary of State, 1995), p. 47.

17. Garrison, *A Treasury of Minnesota Tales*, pp. 168–170.

18. *Hear the Future*, 1996, Minnesota Public Radio capital campaign summary, quoted in Garrison, *A Treasury of Minnesota Tales*, p. 170.

19. U.S. Department of Commerce, U.S. Census Bureau, *1998 Statistical Abstract of the United States* (Washington, DC: U.S. Census Bureau, 1998), p. 12.

20. Garrison, *A Treasury of Minnesota Tales*, p. 7.

21. Diana L. Telschow, State Demographic Center, *Re: Data posted to form 1* (e-mail note to the author), 15 February 2000.

22. "The Land of Good Lessons," p. 28.

23. State of Minnesota, Economic Resource Group, *1998 Economic Report to the Governor* (St. Paul: Offices of the Economic Resource Group, 1998), p. 3.

24. U.S. Department of Commerce, *1998 Statistical Abstract of the United States*, p. 71.

25. Elazar, Gray, and Spano, *Minnesota Politics and Government*, p. 48.

26. Ibid., p. 47.

27. Ibid., p. 46.

28. "Divided We Stand: A Minnesota Poll Report on Shared Values, Social Tolerance, and Community," 2 April 1995, appendix, p. 1, quoted in Elazar, Gray, and Spano, *Minnesota Politics and Government*, pp. 48–49.

29. Elazar, Gray, and Spano, *Minnesota Politics and Government*, p. xxvi.

30. Joseph A. Califano, *Triumph and Tragedy of Lyndon Johnson* (New York: Simon and Schuster, 1991), p. 113.

31. Dane Smith, "Marching to Its Own Drummers," Minneapolis *Star Tribune* Sunday Edition, 15 August 1999, p. A10.

32. Russell Fridley, "Minnesota Has a Long History of Tripartisanship," *St. Paul Pioneer Press* Sunday Edition, 25 July 1999, p. 6A.

33. Lass, *Minnesota: A History*, p. 197.

34. Ibid.

35. Smith, "Marching to Its Own Drummers," p. A10–A11.

36. J. David Gillespie, *Politics at the Periphery* (Columbia: University of South Carolina Press, 1993), p. 245.

37. Lass, *Minnesota: A History*, p. 221.

38. Ibid., p. 222.

39. Gillespie, *Politics at the Periphery*, p. 247.

40. Russell Fridley interview, 2 August 1999.

41. Garrison, *A Treasury of Minnesota Tales*, p. 196.

42. Russell Fridley interview, 2 August 1999.

43. Gillespie, *Politics at the Periphery*, pp. 248–249.

44. Lass, *Minnesota: A History*, p. 229.

45. Smith, "Marching to Its Own Drummers," p. A11.

46. Chris Georgacas, former chairman of the Republican Party of Minnesota and Coleman campaign manager, 4 August 1999, interview by the author, Maplewood, MN.

47. Elazar, Gray, and Spano, *Minnesota Politics and Government*, p. 50.

48. Nick Coleman, "What Does KQ's Success Say About Us?" *St. Paul Pioneer Press*, 18 October 1999, p. 1B.

49. Lass, *Minnesota: A History*, p. 295.

50. Smith, "Marching to Its Own Drummers," p. A11.

51. Elazar, Gray, and Spano, *Minnesota Politics and Government*, p. 24.

52. Ibid., pp. 62–64.

53. Ibid., p. 71.

54. Michael Barone and Grant Ujifusa, *The Almanac of American Politics 1996* (Washington, DC: National Journal Inc., 1995), pp. 723–724.

55. Mary McEvoy, former associate chair of the DFL and Freeman campaign field director, 22 July 1999, telephone interview by the author, Cambridge, MA, to Minneapolis, MN.

56. Elazar, Gray, and Spano, *Minnesota Politics and Government*, p. 71.

57. Smith, "Marching to Its Own Drummers," p. A11.

58. "The Land of Good Lessons," p. 28.

59. Ibid.

60. Elazar describes Minnesota as the epitome a moralistic political culture—cooperative, clean, and well-integrated. He finds this displayed in even small detail, noting that the Minnesota Department of Health once published daily reports of the radiation count. See Daniel J. Elazar, *American Federalism: A View from the States* (New York: Thomas Y. Crowell Company, 1966), pp. 61 and 100.

2

THE 1998 GUBERNATORIAL RACE

The Constructs

In Minnesota the major parties hold conventions every summer. In state election years, the party activists endorse a candidate. However, the endorsing process is just that—an endorsement—until the primary on the Tuesday after the second Monday in September. The primary winner is the actual nominee. The number of delegates to the state endorsing conventions for election years is determined by that party's vote in the previous election. Special spots are reserved for national party members and elected officials. At the June 1998 DFL convention, for example, there were approximately 1,200 alternates. Generally speaking, attendance at endorsing conventions has continually fallen over the years to a point that only the most die-hard activists on either side attend, and, as Carleton College professor of political science Steven Schier puts it, "[The] result is that each party's endorsing convention has become an outpost of exotic politics."[1] The DFL convention in 1998, for example, passed a rule that the event should be "fragrance free," lest somebody's perfume goad somebody else's allergic sensibilities.[2] Dick Senese, a professor at St. Olaf College and former chair of the DFL, laments the corroded convention participation that he thinks undercuts the legitimacy of the endorsement process itself, because then "the decision isn't itself owned by the Democratic Party at large."[3] But DFL activist Kathy Czar describes the process of getting a spot as a delegate as "long and complex"[4]—to do it, party activists must first attend a precinct caucus meeting in early March to run for a slot as a delegate to the county convention in April, and the county units elect delegates to the state convention. The entire process, Czar concedes, is difficult for anyone but a party insider to understand.[5] Thus it is that many people look at an endorsement as something with which they feel no great kinship nor any imposing obligation. A party's nominee is thus not official until the primary election in September, where the small percentage of voters who bother to vote that day choose the person who will become the party's actual candidate, which sometimes causes awkward situations.[6]

Minnesotans do not register as a member of any party and are allowed to vote in the primary for either party, but when they pick up the ballot they must constrain all their votes to one party—they cannot choose a Republican for governor and a Democrat for secretary of state. And so it is not until sometime in September that the general election season actually begins, yielding a situation that is something of a mad dash to the finish.

The Republican Party's Choice: Norm Coleman

The 1998 gubernatorial campaign began, at least for people who pay attention to such things, well over a year before the election with Norm Coleman's reelection as mayor of St. Paul. From that moment on, the gubernatorial race had begun; there was little doubt whether Coleman would run, especially since former party chairman Chris Georgacas had started a movement to draft him for the governor's race when he saw "the writing on the wall" that the mayor had a bright future.[7] The draft letter, sent to 900 activists, described Coleman as "a principled, electable conservative" who possessed "a proven ability to articulate our message and win votes of independents and conservative DFLers."[8] Former congressman Vin Weber put the collective sentiment of many power brokers in the party this way:

> The stars seem to be aligned for him. He's got almost no negatives. He's already incredibly popular. The business community loves him. The national Republican Party loves him. . . . He has the ability to unite the party in the state. He can do it all."[9]

Part of Coleman's appeal to Republicans was that he had switched parties—and so brought with him the aura of a compassionate, good-government-style Minnesota statesman—and had then been reelected in the heavily unionized, heavily DFL capital city with 59 percent of the vote, its first Republican mayor in forty years.[10] With Coleman as mayor, the city's economy improved, crime went down, and the state regained, through his negotiating skills, a national hockey team. He was fresh, able, and full of energy. Governor Arne Carlson liked him, and most of the social conservatives in the party found him acceptable. Most important, he had by far the highest name recognition of possible Republican contenders.[11] He also had the best favorable-unfavorable rating, 60 percent to 6 percent, compared to Lieutenant Governor Benson's 39 percent to 11 percent.[12] It would also be, for Republicans, a pretty great thing to have a Democrat turned Republican capture the governorship of one of the most traditionally Democratic states two years before a presidential election.

It was in this climate that in the middle of February Norm Coleman announced that he was running for governor. He presented himself as a "compassionate conservative" who as governor would be a "salesman, booster, recruiter, whatever it takes, to bring 21st-century jobs to Minnesota."[13] He also unveiled his campaign slogan, "Imagine the Possibilities." (Humphrey's was "Believe in Minnesota," whereas Ventura's was "Retaliate in '98.") Quoting Ronald Reagan, another Democrat turned Republican, he said, "[Nobody] has deeper convictions than a convert." Noting also his conspicuous Brooklyn accent, he said, "I am a Minnesotan not by birth but by choice."[14]

The business community and Republican activists were so fast to join the Coleman bus that on February 24, 1998, almost five months before the convention and seven before the primary, state representative Roy Terwilliger, a respected legislator from Edina, dropped out of the race.[15] That left three Republican candidates—Coleman, Benson, and Allan Quist, a favorite of social conservatives and the 1994 party-endorsed candidate (he lost the primary and the nomination to Carlson). The party chairman, Bill Cooper, was concerned about a fractious GOP endorsing convention and primary contest (such as in 1994), and so he forced the three candidates to sign a pledge that they would not challenge the endorsed candidate in the primary. Cooper later said, "I should point out that as chairman, until a candidate is endorsed, you can't support anyone—but I always thought that Coleman was the most electable candidate."[16] Coleman's name recognition, his history of cutting taxes in St. Paul, and the perception of him as a compassionate conservative—in a race where the two most important issues were taxes and education—were seen as powerful advantages in the general election.

Coleman was not the favorite of strong social conservatives since he was not opposed per se to all government programs, but his pro-life

stance—a good part of the reason he left the DFL—and his commitment
to cutting taxes made him acceptable. Though Chris Georgacas insists
that "contrary to popular opinion, his nomination was not a foregone
conclusion," it was also not an enormous challenge: Jack Meeks, one of
the cofounders of the draft movement, said, "He won the endorsement
on the fourth ballot. Most of Joanne Benson's votes, when she dropped
out, went to Coleman."[17] Cooper explained Coleman's easy victory this
way: "I think the Republican Party activists have become more pragmatic; they agreed with him 80 percent, and they thought he was most
electable."[18] Additionally, said Cooper, "Part of the Republican strategy
was to endorse a candidate, not have a primary, and let the Democrats
have a very divisive primary."[19]

The was little concern aired among Republicans about Coleman's
having switched parties. The move seemed natural: He is pro-life, and
as mayor he refused to endorse a gay pride parade (though he defended
the right of the parade to occur). When he spoke at the 1996 DFL convention, he was greeted with boos. In 1997, Governor Carlson, Vin
Weber, and Chris Georgacas negotiated his party switch.[20] Georgacas
saw it as an honest decision by someone who "felt increasingly uncomfortable in the DFL Party." The Democrats, however, were livid, and
doubly so when he ran for governor. Kathy Czar, a DFL activist, says
that at the DFL convention in 1998, "The overriding concern was beating Norm Coleman."[21] Jann Olsten, who chaired Coleman's gubernatorial campaign kitchen cabinet, described his candidate by saying, "I
liked Norm Coleman because of his energy and his optimism. He's a decent man and has good ideas."[22] Democrat Mary McEvoy, a member of
the state party committee, saw him rather differently: "He's a political
opportunist. He'll sell himself to anyone."[23]

The antipathy among DFLers toward Coleman probably helps explain why GOP hopes for "more of an inter-party play" between the
DFL candidates fell flat. The Democrats all focused their attacks on
Coleman, as evidenced by a radio attack ad run by the DFL against
Coleman in early July.[24] The Democrats ran their own ads against Coleman—the most vigorous was Ted Mondale, son of the former vice president, who continually accused Coleman of supporting the easing of
concealed weapons laws.[25] "We didn't have the Democrats attacking
each other—they all attacked Coleman," remembers Cooper.[26]

Nevertheless, having won the party's endorsement under Cooper's
agreement, Coleman was assured the Republican nomination, whereas
the five Democrats all stayed in the race for the nomination until the
primary on September 15.

The Democratic Farmer-Labor Party Field

The DFL field of candidates was a crowded one. There were three sons of famous Minnesotan politicians running—Hubert "Skip" Humphrey, Ted Mondale, and Mike Freeman, son of Orville Freeman, the former governor and secretary of agriculture in the Kennedy administration. The media uncreatively (but proudly) dubbed them "My Three Sons." In addition, a fourth heir to power was running: Mark Dayton, department store heir, who elegantly shattered fundraising records by writing himself a $1.8 million check.[27] Dayton also had the distinction of being called by a TV news profile four days before the primary "the least at ease of the DFL candidates."[28] The field was rounded out by state senator Doug Johnson of Tower (in the Iron Range, in the northern part of the state), chairman of the Senate Tax Committee whose own father was a welder.[29] Johnson stood out because he was the only candidate from outside the Twin Cities, a man of actual humble origins, and the only pro-life DFL candidate (representing the more conservative, rural DFL base). Johnson is an angler and a hunter, and in the senate he lambasted proposals for tax-funded Twin Cities sports stadiums as an unjust cost to the rural parts of the state. He was counting on the support of the union, conservative, blue-collar, outlying voters to win the primary.[30] He also stood out from the rest not just for his totally genuine "common touch" but for his considerable girth.

Ted Mondale, like Johnson, believes that the Democratic Farmer-Labor Party is dominated by doctrinaire, intolerant activists. Mondale is only partly his father's son. He certainly seems like his father in his youth—handsome and possessed of an interest in politics and a concern for people. But he considers himself a "New Democrat" and wants to help steer the DFL Party, stubbornly liberal as ever, to the political center. "If I got up at the DFL convention and said, for example, that I thought that welfare reform, something that has been accepted by Democrats in other states, was a good thing, I'd get booed off the stage," he says.[31] From time to time one can hear the two Mondales, Walter and Ted, on Minnesota Public Radio, arguing over public policy, the son staking out a position defiantly to the right of his father. A large part of his proposed budget was cutting needless programs; one of his favorite vignettes is of setting out to reform the Metropolitan Mosquito Control District (charged with controlling the mind-crushing horror that is the mosquito population) and finding that during the winter, employees of the agency went to school districts to warn them about malaria.[32] Because of the relative unpopularity of his views among hard-core DFLers, he, like Johnson, placed his bets on the primary. Mike Freeman said this of him: "The worst thing that Ted Mondale did was to legitimize a son of the founder of the party—Humphrey—running in the primary against an endorsed candidate. If both a Humphrey and a Mondale could run against the party, then the endorsement really didn't mean a lot."[33]

The Endorsement and the Primary

The DFL endorsing convention narrowly selected Freeman as the endorsed candidate. Humphrey's advantages were mainly his high name recognition and polls showing him as the only Democrat able to defeat Norm Coleman in the general election. Freeman's advantages were that he had been campaigning for the endorsement since 1994, that he had locked up endorsements from nearly every traditional interest group, and that he impressed the conventioneers by being the only candidate to promise to withdraw from the race if he lost the endorsement race.[34] And, since the choice seemed to be really between these two, Freeman also benefited from concern among party insiders over the potential for a repeat of Skip Humphrey's failed 1988 U.S. Senate campaign.[35]

Dick Senese, a member of the party's executive committee, said of the situation, "It's fair to say that a majority of the executive committee supported Freeman."[36] Mary McEvoy, eventual outreach director of Freeman's campaign after he won the endorsement, said, "I was impressed with how he united the party. I liked his positions on education, both elementary and higher education. And he got started four years earlier, so he was up and running."[37] Humphrey, by contrast, received tepid support from key constituencies from whom Freeman had won endorsements. He was seen as more of an upstart who perhaps did not have the best interests of the party at heart.[38] And as Freeman put it, "It was my turn."[39]

Ted Mondale and Doug Johnson made only a nominal appearance at the convention, knowing that their relatively conservative stances stood a better chance in the primary.[40] Mark Dayton made an earnest attempt at the convention but evoked little sympathy.[41] Freeman narrowly won on the tenth ballot (60 percent was needed to claim victory). He recalled bitterly, "At the convention I was leading with 50 percent or more after the second ballot. However, the Humphrey campaign refused to concede even after I got 59.6 percent. I believe that by pushing the convention to ten ballots and going after 10 p.m. they generated such ill will that it cost him much-needed party support in the general election."[42] Freeman was offended, not only personally but also because he felt himself to be the stronger general election candidate:

> I think there were fairly significant issue differences between Skip and me, but the big question was, who could beat Norm Coleman? Skip had the tobacco settlement [which gave him an early lead in general election polls] . . . versus Mike Freeman, who has strong party support, is a hard worker for the party, and has stronger support from virtually every constituency—feminists, gays and lesbians, trade unions, and farmers.[43]

In Freeman's eyes, Humphrey had a single advantage over him: "Skip's whole campaign was built on being a winner."

In terms of choosing a nominee, the endorsing convention was completely ineffectual. The entire DFL field remained in the race for the nomination, and the endorsed candidate did not get noted as such on the primary ballot. Paul Wellstone made several appearances for Mike Freeman, and the DFL ran some ads for him, including vague radio spots on education—"zero tolerance" for violence in schools and the need to "involve parents"—and tax cuts, so that Minnesotans could reinvest money "where it belongs—in our families."[44] Humphrey and the rest of the field continued to campaign themselves, undeterred, and the polls, both for the primary and in general election match-ups, showed Humphrey as the clear favorite.[45]

The DFL's Choice: Hubert Horatio Humphrey III

Hubert Horatio "Skip" Humphrey III inherited a family tradition of public service and a name that one of his DFL rivals called "platinum." As scion of Minnesota's most revered political family, he had served as the state's attorney general since 1982, for which he was well regarded for championing popular consumer issues. The high point of his career was his leadership in filing suit against the tobacco companies, leading to a settlement that brought $6 billion to the state's coffers. Humphrey was and is steadfastly committed to the ideal of public service, and he was deeply proud to have had "the honor of serving the people of Minnesota for sixteen years as attorney general."[46] He is also, as a *St. Paul Pioneer Press* staff editorial put it, "an old-fashioned liberal who believes in government." He deeply believes that government can do good things for people. In his speech at the DFL convention, he promised

> As your governor, I will stand shoulder-to-shoulder with working fam-
> ilies—to raise the minimum wage, fight for a living wage and enforce
> the prevailing wage. For every child, quality health care. For every re-
> tiree, a secure pension. And for every working family, a tax cut to
> make ends meet.[47]

He also promised to lower class sizes, hire more teachers, provide two
years of postsecondary education, and provide increased early child-
hood programs. Such an apostle of this worldview is he that his original
budget plan for his hypothetical governorship had to be toned down
when Ted Mondale pointed out that it had "a billion dollar hole."[48]

Early polls of theoretical general election match-ups had Humphrey
beating Coleman, 44 percent to 34 percent, making him the only Democrat polling ahead of Coleman (Mike Freeman was next closest, polling
31 percent in a theoretical contest with Coleman). In the same poll Jesse
Ventura got just 10 percent of the vote in a Humphrey-Coleman match-
up, and slightly more in contests with different opponents.[49]

That the eventual nominees were Skip Humphrey and Norm Coleman guaranteed a bitter and emotional contest. Coleman had, in fact,
worked for Skip in the attorney general's office. They were tight
friends; some say that Coleman regarded Humphrey as a father. Coleman had been the rising star at the attorney general's office, where he
often wrote speeches for his boss. And now strings of circumstance had
aligned in form, depositing the two of them to face each other in an
election they would both lose.

Birthing the Minnesota Reform Party

In July 1992, the Minnesota for Perot group had a meeting at the VFW
building in Bloomington (a Minneapolis suburb) after Ross Perot with-
drew from the race for president. Dean Barkley, the man who eventually
convinced Jesse Ventura to run, remembers: "Everyone was wondering
what we should do now that Perot was gone. During the meeting, Phil
Madsen got up and stated what was obvious to me—that we needed to
start a new political party. I became the second member."[50] Madsen
gives a similar account: "I got up and said, 'What we need to do is start
a political party.'" The Minnesota Independence Party was born. The
Reform Party label was adopted in 1996, when Ross Perot ran again.

The party's first victory came in 1993 when it helped Steve Minn
win a nonpartisan Minneapolis City Council seat from the thirteenth
district.[51] Barkley had run for Congress as an Independent in 1992, was

endorsed by the Minneapolis *Star Tribune*, and participated in the debates, winning 17 percent of the vote.[52] He ran for Senate in 1994 against Rod Grams and Ann Wynia and again in 1996 against Paul Wellstone and Rudy Boschwitz, winning 5 percent and 7 percent, respectively.[53] Barkley first met Jesse Ventura in 1994 when the Reform Party met to endorse Governor Carlson, whose pro-choice stance had kept him from his own party's endorsement. Barkley remembers that

> Jesse had been very fair to me by talking about my campaign on his [radio] show. . . . In '96 I asked him if he would be my honorary chair, basically to get him to walk in some parades for me. . . . During the 4th of July parade in Annandale, he walked with me, and that was when I first saw the "Ventura Mystique." He had the whole crowd chanting "Jesse!" even though it was my hometown.[54]

As the parade rolled along and people continued their enthusiasm for the former wrestler, radio talk show host, and part-time movie star, Barkley had a revelation. He turned to Ventura and said, "Jesse, the wrong guy's running."[55]

Barkley convinced Ventura to appear at the Reform Party booth at the 1997 Minnesota State Fair, where "he was very well received." Throughout the eighteen months before the election, Barkley, Madsen, and Doug Friedline, another key party activist, continually hounded Jesse, who was reluctant to run.[56] "I called him every two weeks for six months," recalls Friedline.[57] Eventually, Ventura asked them to meet at his horse ranch. Barkley recalls this first meeting and the first subject Ventura wanted to discuss: "He wanted to know about the disgusting process of asking for money and how degrading that is. I told him." Ventura seemed to be coming around to the idea of running, but he had to convince his wife, Terry. "Terry did not want him to do it," remembers Barkley, and so Ventura "gave her the American Dream speech."[58] Eventually, reluctantly, Mrs. Ventura gave in, and the Ventura for Governor campaign was launched.

The Body, Stage Right

Jesse Ventura—one-time U.S. Navy SEAL[59] and professional wrestler, short-lived actor in *Predator*, former mayor of a Minneapolis suburb, AM radio talk show host—became a candidate for governor of the state of Minnesota on January 26, 1998, when he stood on the steps of the

State Capitol and announced his candidacy by declaring, "If I fail . . . then the American dream is dead."[60]

The Reform Party activists began plotting. "We knew we had to get Jesse into Perot range—low-to-mid-twenties in the polls—by October of 1998 while spending as little money as possible," explains Barkley.[61] To this end, they utilized the free-of-cost "Ventura Mystique" by putting Ventura in front of the public whenever and wherever they could ("I think he was grand marshal of twelve parades," remembers Barkley).

Still, Ventura's popularity did not translate into a perceived ability to lead. Ventura had 64 percent name recognition, and he assumed that such a number was unambiguously positive for his campaign.[62] He failed to notice, however, that in the same poll he held a favorable-unfavorable rating of 23 percent to 27 percent.[63]

On February 3, 1998, the *Star Tribune* reported on the fundraising progress of those in the race. Hubert Humphrey had raised over $260,000, Mike Freeman over $230,000, and Ted Mondale over $365,000. Republicans Joanne Benson and Norm Coleman (who had not yet announced his candidacy) had raised $235,000 and $113,000, respectively. Jesse Ventura had raised $1,195.[64]

Ventura faced no opposition for the Reform Party endorsement, and at the Reform Party nominating convention on June 6, he officially accepted their nomination. Ventura's speech was, as usual, composed of his thoughts as they occurred to him on the spot. Ventura does his spontaneous speechifying in part because he believes it is more honest; at one debate a woman offered him a legal pad for notes, but he refused, telling her that "if you tell the truth then you don't need any notes."[65] Compounding his ad hoc way of speaking is grammar that somehow never quite compares in quality to what he means to say. Confident as ever, he told the delegates: "We can win. And we can win governor. I was very much encouraged by the polls lately. . . . We're only averaging like 16 percent right now. . . . Well, first of all, I don't buy those polls." Then he made a remarkably accurate prediction for his campaign: "We have only one direction to go, and that is up."[66]

When he officially filed for governor on Monday, July 25, his employer, AM talk radio station KFAN, pulled him from the air, out of fairness to the other candidates.[67] Ventura was angered by the station's act—and so, apparently missing the point, he began challenging the other candidates to stop accepting their government paychecks while campaigning.

The Campaign Heats Up

During the summer of 1998 the campaign for governor shifted into high gear. Coleman locked up the Republican nomination in early June, and Freeman won the DFL Party's endorsement. But it was Ventura who first demonstrated his signature campaign platform on a large scale at the Minnesota Citizens' Forum, a statewide nonpartisan gathering of hundreds of citizens that is sponsored by numerous civic and media organizations.[68] Coleman, Ventura, and the DFL candidates all attended, and the focus was on taxes. Coleman spoke first, describing Minnesotans as having "one of the highest tax burdens in the country" and himself as "the only candidate in this race who has actually cut taxes as a chief executive" (as mayor of St. Paul). Freeman laid out a 20 percent tax cut for homeowners and renters, proceeding to offer his reasoning behind this (these people are "the backbone" of communities), and he suggested limiting the break to $1,000 "so that it benefits working families and senior citizens." Mark Dayton did not mention tax cuts but instead gave a two-paragraph description of what a "surplus" actually is, seeming to suggest it was much different from and less than what a surplus was being made out to be, and at some point he promised that there would be no new spending if he were elected and that all unexpected "surpluses" would be heading directly into a public savings account. Ted Mondale began by declaring his belief in the straightforward idea that "Minnesotans are taxed too much." He offered a cut in sales taxes and emphasized his antipathy for government inefficiency and waste. Doug Johnson said that he himself was "the only candidate to propose a permanent income tax cut." He wanted property tax cuts that would total $400 million. Skip Humphrey stated that the "first priority of the current budget surplus ought to be to return a substantial amount to the working families in this state"; he then said that the $6 billion coming from the tobacco companies would allow the state to cut taxes "responsibly." He proposed $2 billion in "targeted" income tax cuts for "working families" and promised to work with the legislature to reform "Minnesota's unfair property-tax system."

Jesse Ventura began his own response, which was delivered among all the other candidates' budget-theorizing and number-crunching, with six unambiguous words in three sentences: "Cut taxes. Cut taxes. Cut taxes." Deriding any system that would allow "$4 billion in surpluses," he suggested abandoning the income tax in favor of a consumption tax, saying that the government needed to stop "penalizing people for working and

saving money."[69] He proposed a law that "automatically triggers the return of all surplus funds to the people whose money produced the surplus." He declared himself "the only major gubernatorial candidate who
has called for a full return of the surplus to the taxpayers" and con-
cluded with a rhetorical flourish: "Who do you trust more to keep your
money in your hands, Jesse Ventura or the career politicians?"[70]

In late July the *Star Tribune* ran one of its first major stories on
Ventura. It focused on his common-man-style wooing of veterans at an
American Legion hall. In it, one of his supporters, a former Marine,
says, "Jesse alienates a lot of people, but he's got great ideas and he'd
get things done. So what if wrestling's just an act—politics is a bigger
act than wrestling." Ventura announced to those present,

> I'm going to fool everyone in this race like I fooled them on the one in
> Brooklyn Park [a suburb where he held a weak mayorship in the early
> 1990s]. . . . Look, 45 percent of Minnesotans don't vote—and we're
> good in this state. I can get 20 percent of them to vote this one time and
> watch your vote count. Rest assured, I can get the other 20 percent. And
> in a three-candidate race, 40 percent wins. Forget about "My Three
> Sons," the rich guy [Dayton] and the guy up north [Johnson].[71]

Mayor Coleman first stumbled in August when he waffled on his
concealed weapon position. He had, in his zeal to prove his new conservative credentials and win the GOP endorsement in June, supported
a statewide, uniform standard by which citizens could get a concealed-
carry permit (currently, the issuance of permits is done at the individual—and some say arbitrary—discretion of local police chiefs) in his
speech at the Republican convention. (Indeed, some high-ranking Republicans confided that they thought this was the exact issue that lost
Coleman the election, because it left many otherwise Republican voters uncomfortable with his positions.) At a news conference on June 13,
after numerous attack ads on the subject by the Democrats, he offered
a "clarification," saying that to get such a permit, a person would have
to show an occupational or "personal safety hazard," the interpretation
of which would still be up to local police departments.[72]

Of course everyone pounced. Freemen and the other DFL candidates attacked him for two things: backing away from his original position, and supporting looser concealed-carry laws in the first place.
Knowing that the issue was a clear threat to Coleman among the suburban "soccer moms," the DFL ran a radio spot claiming (wrongly) that
Coleman wanted "to allow virtually any adult to carry a concealed gun
to a mall, a movie theater, even a kids' soccer game." The Gun Owners

Civil Rights League was equally indignant; David Gross, a board member, said, "I am personally embarrassed by this, and I thought he had more spine."[73]

Of course, Coleman had originally said that he supported creating a statewide standard of "personal or occupational hazard"; that is, unifying the criteria one would have to pass in order to be allowed to carry a gun. Not particularly interested in that nuance, the Democrats gleefully leapt at the chance to paint a horrifying picture for the public, and Coleman had to return to allowing local police departments discretion, for fear of losing his moderate support.[74]

FarmFest

Things were still waiting to worsen for Norm Coleman. Each year Minnesota's farmers get together in the southwestern part of the state for FarmFest, during which they talk shop, check out new equipment, have livestock shows and cookouts, and so forth. It is traditional for political candidates to come down and make an appearance, and Republican candidates usually fare well, as this is a strong GOP base.[75] Coleman's appearance, however, amounted to shooting himself in the foot: Before a crowd in the midst of a farm crisis and already slightly suspicious of his big-city style, his strange accent, and his fancy suits, he garbled his syntax in an answer to a question, saying "It's not just about this image of what the family farm was and that we're going to save it defies economic reality."[76]

Later, he would spend much of his campaign apologizing and insisting that he was not saying anything negative about the family farm, but to family farmers it certainly seemed that he did. They were unhappy, to put it mildly. State Demographer Tom Gillaspy remembers arriving at FarmFest immediately after the candidates' speeches:

> I came along afterwards. I asked what they thought of the candidates' forum, and the people I talked to were fairly upset with what he had said. They indicated that they were traditional Republicans, and they really questioned whether they could vote that way [now]. When I asked who looked good among the candidates, they all said the same thing, using basically the same words: "You're not going to believe this, but . . . Jesse Ventura." They seemed almost apologetic in a way.[77]

Ventura's campaign secretary remembered it well: "When Jesse met people, they loved him. The farm people just absolutely fell in love with him. . . . [He] went down to FarmFest and he zonked the other candidates. My cousin [a farmer] said, 'He's a good man. He's just good simple folk. We like simple, honest folk.'"[78]

The DFL seized the moment and began running a TV ad that featured a farmer from Randolph named Doug Felton saying, "I know Norm Coleman is wrong to write off the family farm. After all, even in the global economy, people have to eat."[79] Coleman never fully recovered from his gaffe.

In August the GOP began running anti-Humphrey radio spots talking about Coleman's record of cutting taxes and crime and welfare in St. Paul, and his plans for safer schools and permanent tax cuts. A simultaneous ad talked about Skip Humphrey's past votes (from 25 years ago) to decriminalize drugs (small amounts of marijuana) and reduce sentences for murder; the ad suggested that his "failed philosophy from the past" would require higher taxes. The first ad, initially seeming like a positive ad for Coleman rather than a negative ad against Humphrey, nevertheless ended with a swipe at the Humphrey name itself and a flourish: "Coleman . . . not a name from the past."[80] In fact, the DFL and Republican ads were the first skirmishes in the major party battle that would confer a de facto statesman-like aura to Ventura.

The Great Minnesota Get-Together

According to the state demographer, in July 1998 Minnesota's population was 4,725,000, making it the twenty-sixth most populous state in the nation.[81] Additionally, Minnesota has the country's third-largest state fair; in 1999, somewhere on the order of 1.644 million people (mostly Minnesotans) attended, which means that about a third of Minnesota's citizens came to the state fair.[82] "The Great Minnesota Get-Together" goes on for two weeks at the end of the summer just before Labor Day. There is an extensive agricultural element, with everything from different barns for various livestock displayed handsomely in glorious clouds of smells to an agricultural seed exhibit that includes artwork created thereof. You can get all the milk you can drink for a quarter. Many of the state's television and radio stations make a point of broadcasting from the fair during its run. Minnesota-based corporations such as 3M set up booths and give away promotional items. There are rides, the same each year, which is disconcerting only to those too old to enjoy them but old enough to remember that the same rickety structures were there in their own youth. There is a selection of not just greasy food staples but also the latest in foods-on-sticks (fried pickle on a stick, egg roll on a stick). The fair is hot, humid, smelly—and everyone goes. Of course, politicians always have booths. And Jesse Ventura had a booth.

Ventura had an inexpensive opportunity to reach—and charm—a large percentage of the state's voters on an individual level. His booth was almost always swamped with people who may have been less excited about his candidacy than the entertainment value of his green and black "Ventura for Governor" bumper stickers and black T-shirts with "Retaliate in '98" written across the chest in neon-green lettering. (Indeed, of the approximately $300,000 the campaign raised in private donations, Phil Madsen estimates that fully half of it came from T-shirt sales.)[83]

But regardless of why other people were there, Jesse Ventura was there, sharing nuggets of political wisdom and radiating pure populism. "I don't believe in politics, I believe in results," he quipped.[84] His own political ideology seemed to be largely libertarian: fewer taxes, less government, more freedom, more individual responsibility. "I will veto any new taxes that come on my desk," he could be heard promising.[85] Asking a man whom one might reasonably suspect of owning a Harley if he indeed owned a Harley and receiving an affirmative answer, Ventura responded, "Rest assured, I'll veto any helmet law—that's your option." To those who listened, he gave his opinion on the perception that a vote for a third party is wasted, saying, "I find that to be utterly pompous."[86]

Ventura never hesitated to argue with potential voters, as he did with a man over a proposal to build a light-rail transit system from the suburbs into the Twin Cities as a way to alleviate the increasingly congested traffic.[87] The man thought it was a bad idea, and Ventura shot back, "If we don't do it, look at the future like LA."[88]

Ted Mondale was at his own booth, campaigning for the DFL nomination, and said of Ventura, "This guy worked insanely hard. I was at the state fair campaigning, and Jesse was always there, from morning till night."[89] Dane Smith, a longtime Twin Cities political reporter, remembered Ventura's performance as the first time he took serious notice of the man: "I noticed Jesse's magnetic appeal at the state fair. He was the know-nothing every-guy. Everywhere he went at the state fair, he was surrounded by people longing to be near him."[90] Many fairgoers were less interested in policy than in Jesse himself, and he spent a good amount of his time talking wrestling, explaining why his favorite movie was *Jaws* and not *Full Metal Jacket* (in which he appeared), and what it was like to be a Navy SEAL.[91] There were young people, visibly too young to vote, who flocked to see him; a TV story on the candidate showed three screaming teenage girls, one of whom yelled into the camera, "I was screaming and then we came and we saw this guy and we're like, oh I know Jesse the Body! And it was really cool."[92] Campaign workers passed out "Jesse Dollars," oversized fake bills with Jesse's mug in place of Washington's. They passed out nearly 8,000 green and black bumper stickers, frequently running out because of their popularity, and over 6,000 buttons.[93] The state fair also gave a huge boost to the popularity of "Retaliate in '98" T-shirts, which were later sold over the Internet and at all campaign events. Ventura informed fairgoers and reporters alike that he was no longer "The Body." He was, he told them, now "The Mind," because "I make my living with my mind now, not my body, so I'm Jesse 'The Mind.'" He was, he announced, mentally body-slamming people now. Asked if that might be a disappointment to some of his fans, he replied that he didn't think so, "'cause I still got eighteen-inch pipes."

Perhaps most important, Ventura's popularity at the fair convinced Bill Hillsman, the ad guru who would eventually join Ventura's campaign, that Ventura had a chance to win and was worth Hillsman's energy. Nevertheless, despite his booth's overwhelming success, a poll released at the end of the fair by the *Pioneer Press* had Ventura still in the low double digits, at 13 percent, trailing Humphrey's 43 percent and Coleman's 29 percent.[94]

Early in September, the candidates, especially the multiple Democrats still gunning in the primary, eagerly weighed in on the Northwest Airlines pilots' strike. Mike Freeman asked Northwest executives to stop taking paychecks while the strikers did without. Johnson wanted the ads on both sides stopped so that the business of negotiating could get going. Skip Humphrey suggested that Northwest—known as Northworst to many Minnesotans—might get its act together if there were more competition for the airline's semi-monopoly on the state's air travel. Mondale concurred. Coleman lamented the politicizing of the issue, saying the main concern was to get people talking again. Ventura was the only one with a specific plan: locking both sides in a room, surrounding the building with National Guard troops, and giving them a supply of C-rations with the ultimatum that "you're remaining there until you solve it, one way or another."[95]

A week before the DFL primary, the candidates were out and about trying to corral labor votes. Humphrey's campaign enjoyed a visit from Iowa Senator Tom Harkin, while Doug Johnson chose a populist drive on a four-wheeler at a Labor Day parade. Mondale and Dayton likewise attended local parades and events, while Freeman, at a picnic with AFL-CIO brass, gave an indication of how devalued the endorsing process had become, declaring, "This is a referendum on the DFL endorsement system, and on the strength of organized labor."[96] It was a referendum he lost.

The Primaries

Skip Humphrey, Norm Coleman, and Jesse Ventura won nominations in the September 15 primary. Coleman had the benefit of the gentleman's agreement to honor the endorsing process, so he ran essentially unopposed, garnering 91 percent of the primary vote against token opposition, a disgruntled St. Paul homeowner. Ventura likewise ran unopposed and presciently proclaimed that "November 4th, there's going to be crow served to a lot of people."

Unlike Coleman and Ventura, the contest that Humphrey won was bitter. The weekend before the primary, the DFL candidates barnstormed through the state, looking to pick up voters where they felt they could get them best (Humphrey in Duluth, Freeman in the Iron Range, Dayton in downtown Minneapolis, Johnson in Little Falls, Mondale in a suburb). An indication that the DFL party apparatus was upset at Humphrey was a DFL radio ad for Freeman that featured Paul Wellstone talking about how he himself had once been the underdog in his own race.[97]

Humphrey won the primary for a host of reasons. First, a lot of support that might have gone to Freeman was spread around because of the crowded field. Freeman explained,

> One of the reasons I lost is that there were five people running. Most of the people who voted for Mark Dayton were liberal. I would have gotten two out of three of those votes. In a similar fashion, Doug Johnson got the sportsman vote. I was the only sportsman in this race other than Doug. Give me six of ten of Johnson's support and I'm up near 40 percent—and you've got one hell of a tight race.[98]

Moreover, interest and participation in the party primaries had been declining for years, and this year's was a record low turnout. The *Pioneer Press* reported on the day after the primary that many who voted were motivated more by a sense of civic duty than by an interest in any candidate in particular.[99] And these people were probably distracted. As Ted Mondale put it, "There were three things going on at the time. First, the impeachment in Washington. Second, the Northwest strike. And third, a farm crisis. People were not paying as much attention to the election here, and Humphrey's name was enough to put him over the top."[100] Likewise, Mondale believes that the media's promoting the "My Three Sons" theme resulted in a blurring of distinctions between the DFL candidates and left many voters relatively unaware of important differences between them. In the end, Skip's last name, and its remaining legacy of the 1960s and 1970s, was probably unbeatable; as Mike Freeman said, "Sometimes, particularly when I was in senior citizen centers, it seemed as if I were running against the former Vice President and not Skip."[101] (It's notable that senior citizens tend to vote in primary elections at much higher rates than other age groups.)

This is not to undercut Humphrey's win or his impressive record as a public servant. He had been a diligent and effective attorney general who brought the state the $6 billion tobacco settlement. He had held a statewide office for sixteen years and enjoyed a genuine following all his own. And, perhaps most important of all, he was the only Democratic candidate whom polling showed as capable of winning over Coleman.

The Games Begin

The general election campaign season thus began in mid-September, barely a month and a half before the final votes would be counted. The first day was a hurricane of activity. It featured a Republican operative at a Humphrey news conference dressed in a chicken suit and carrying a sign reading "Quit Skipping Debates," a play on Humphrey's nickname and a reference to his cancellation of a Minnesota Chamber of Commerce debate in favor of taking a trip to Duluth to receive the endorsement of organized labor.

In Duluth, the AFL-CIO switched its endorsement from Freeman to Humphrey. "I don't like to be outside. I like to be inside. I thank you for inviting me into your house of labor," quipped an ebullient Humphrey, who also at one point said, "This is the way our future's going to be—bright and sunny."[102] He declared, "You're not a special interest—you're in the public interest."

The same day, Norm Coleman appealed to his constituency, talking at the Minnesota Chamber of Commerce and painting Humphrey as a tax-and-spend liberal who would raise taxes to pay for his big governmental programs. "His own DFL opponents said that," Coleman said. Governor Carlson debuted as a Coleman campaign surrogate, giving a speech as well in which he took Coleman's criticism of Humphrey to a much more vivid level, saying that the DFLer "has the same propensity toward spending as a dog has for a fire hydrant . . . an irresistible force." He added, "If Norm Coleman loses, every person in this room, including myself, loses."[103] Business leaders feared a Humphrey victory; indeed, the event at which Coleman and Carlson spoke was to be a debate for the primary winners, but after Humphrey backed out, the event became a spirited pro-Coleman rally. Business leaders still remembered the attorney general's "stings" from six years before wherein he set up a fake company called Red Lion to solicit small businesses and offer to dispose of their waste on the cheap and in ostensible violation of environmental dumping laws.[104] They also worried that a DFL governor and legislature (both houses of which were controlled by the DFL) would revoke the 1995 overhaul of the state's workers' compensation system, a change that business leaders say not only saved them money but their companies as well.[105]

The same day, Humphrey depicted a similarly apocalyptic vision of a Coleman administration, where everyone carries handguns and small family farms are run out of business. The Republican Party again aired the ad on Humphrey's vote in the state senate to soften laws on marijuana (25 years before), and Humphrey counterattacked at a news conference by pointing out Coleman's own drug use as a hippie at Woodstock (28 years before). Jesse Ventura spent the day coaching high school football, as he did every day, as a volunteer.

On the second day of the general election season Norm Coleman promised to cut income taxes, eliminate the marriage penalty, and allow farmers to skip their 1999 property tax payments, all of which amounted to a three-year, $3 billion plan of tax cuts. To a state with the second-highest income tax in the country, Coleman explained, "Cutting taxes is like watering your garden. It makes it grow." Coleman's across-the-board plan for tax cuts put him in stark contrast to Humphrey's plan, which planned $1.4 billion in cuts over four years. The Humphrey plan not only cut taxes by a smaller amount but also consisted largely of targeted property tax cuts for lower-income families and tax credits for elderly care, higher education, and child care; the only unilateral cut in Humphrey's plan was for the lowest tax bracket, affecting the first $25,000 of income in a family, saving an average family $100 a year, compared to the approximately $400 they would get with Coleman's plan. Humphrey described Coleman's plan as "irresponsible"; Coleman taunted Humphrey's focus on working families, saying, "We take a broader, more realistic definition of working families."[106]

The *Pioneer Press* featured an article during this first week that cast Ventura as a spoiler for Coleman.[107] The same day, a second article discussed many of the hurdles facing Coleman in the coming general election, which included the "Jesse factor," a deficit to Humphrey in the polls, difficulty building trust with rural voters, and his unpopular support of using public money for a new Twin Cities sports stadium. One St. Paul resident was quoted as saying, "We didn't like Coleman, we didn't like him pushing that stadium down out throats." A *Pioneer Press* editorial in the September 8 sports section detailed the explosiveness of the stadium issue. Skip Humphrey was vocally opposed to any public funding. Coleman, who earnestly believed building a stadium was a good investment that would generate income, tried to remain ambiguously in favor of different levels of public support, often suggesting "user fees"—taxes on tickets and parking. Still, as the article pointed out, a loosely knit group of citizens were working for support of a new ballpark and could not give away their endorsement—nobody wanted it.[108]

That Friday, Jesse Ventura strode onto the scene in full force for the first time. At the Governor's Economic Summit, the Republican and DFL candidates were both invited to address the conference. Ventura was omitted, or may have been omitted—it's unclear. After he showed up anyway, a last-minute offer to speak was turned down, probably because he knew the value of a dramatic entrance. State Senate Majority Leader Roger Moe, Humphrey's running mate, used his allotted time to make some short, perfunctory remarks about the Humphrey-Moe vision for Minnesota and then yielded his remaining time to Ventura after announcing the Humphrey campaign would not participate in any debates in which Ventura was not included—their strategy being to help Ventura's fiscal conservatism siphon away Republican voters from Coleman. Ventura strode to the podium in a camouflage jacket, hiking boots, and the hat he had worn in the movie *Predator* and began his remarks with galactic understatement: "You're going to find me a little different from the other candidates."[109]

Dick Senese, a member of the DFL executive committee, remembers, "We had this 'everyone grab hands, link arms' thing that Saturday, but it was mostly for show. I don't think Mike Freeman really did much [for the Humphrey campaign] after that."[110]

The next day's *Pioneer Press* featured a staff editorial that opened with the declaration that "Minnesota voters have a clear choice in the general election contest for governor—between DFL and Republican candidates with sharply contrasting styles, priorities, and philosophies of government." There was no mention of the Reform Party; most polls at this time had Ventura stuck around 10 percent. First describing Humphrey as "an unrepentant '70s liberal who is not shy about using government power and resources to solve problems" and who "made one expensive promise after another in an effort to win" that he then had to cut back, the paper declared that he "needs to demonstrate he is serious about keeping the state's budget in balance, that he knows how to establish priorities and make tough choices." It then discussed Coleman's self-described "substantial, permanent tax cut," his belief in expanding school choice, and his anticrime plans as "the kind of bold leadership he has brought to St. Paul," then added, "That's a start, but voters deserve more details about Coleman's vision for Minnesota. They also deserve to know how far Coleman would go to deliver on commitments made to hard-line conservatives during the GOP endorsement process—to relax restrictions on the carrying of concealed weapons, repeal human rights protections for gays and restrict abortion rights." The final two-sentence paragraph is devoted to Jesse Ventura, dismissively saying, "He needs to offer a comprehensive vision for the state—to demonstrate that he is a serious candidate and not merely trying to boost his [radio show] ratings."[111]

The already heated battle worsened that weekend. There was supposed to be a cease-fire in the ad war following the death of Muriel Humphrey-Brown, Skip's mother, but a "communication breakdown" resulted in the state GOP airing ads that weekend (the Coleman campaign itself did not air any ads that weekend). This offended the DFL, or at least gave it an excuse for a display of some anger. Of course, the DFL was simultaneously preparing anti-Coleman ads to begin the next Monday. Norm Coleman, who had worked for Skip in the attorney general's office and knew the extended Humphrey family, attended the service.[112] Eventually, in time for the funeral on Tuesday, both sides had pulled their respective ads.[113]

Things seemed to keep getting worse for Coleman. The Minneapolis *Star Tribune* released a poll on September 23 that had him trailing Humphrey 49 percent to 29 percent. Ventura came in at 10 percent.[114] With this as a backdrop, the *Pioneer Press* featured an article the next day called "Humphrey, Coleman Wary of 'Everyman' Ventura." It was not particularly prescient, mostly casting Ventura as a spoiler for Coleman, but it was remarkably laudatory of Ventura, drawing links between his "working class roots" and his appeal to ordinary people sick of regular politicians.[115] The article included anecdotes from his supporters, who said things such as "Jesse's not a career politician, and he knows what people out here in civilian life are going through" and "Jesse represents the regular guy who is not indebted to special interests."[116]

In late September, the Coleman campaign began running a radio ad in rural areas in which he spoke to farmers directly, trying to undo the image of his being out of touch with rural Minnesota:

> We didn't have a lot, growing up. I was one of eight kids. My dad lost his business. We lost our homes. I had to go to work to help out. My name is Norm Coleman. I know what farmers are going through. And you know you can't believe everything you hear in the media. So please understand this: I am committed to the family farm.

Coleman then lists his support of family farmers, his proposed 50 percent cut in 1999 property taxes, his opposition to a livestock moratorium, and workers' comp reform.[117]

The lull in fighting following the death of Mrs. Humphrey came to a sharp end on the last Sunday in September, when Norm Coleman stood on the steps of the State Capitol and signed a Taxpayers League of Minnesota pledge that he would not raise taxes as governor, saying, "This race for governor is really about who's going to cut your taxes. I will. And about who is going to raise your taxes—Skip Humphrey will." Humphrey, who did not sign the pledge, held a news conference to lament Coleman's "stealing" of a billion dollars of his tobacco settlement for tax cuts, protesting that "he's stealing it from the kids."[118]

On September 28, Arne Carlson presented Coleman with a mock veto pen about six feet tall. "Arne, your path is my path," Coleman said in reference to Carlson's having penned more vetoes (of spending bills) than all governors before him combined.[119]

Within the next few days Jesse and running mate Mae Schunk, a 63-year-old St. Paul public school teacher, proposed the centerpiece of their education plan: smaller class sizes. This would be achieved easily by enforcing "a current law that requires 17-1 [student/teacher ratio] in Minnesota education today," said Schunk. The state was currently achieving a 19-1 ratio. Neither of them offered a way to fund those smaller classes; the Minnesota Education Association estimated the tab of getting the ratio down in grades from kindergarten to third grade at $113 million. The law is also more vague than Ventura and Schunk made it seem—it required the ratio "on average" from K-6 and "as revenue is available."[120] What's interesting is that the paper reported these details only once and let it go after that. Coleman and Humphrey, per usual, did not respond to Ventura, in part out of fear of legitimizing him and in part because they were so focused on attacking each other.

An event in early October provides a good illustration of the degree to which Ventura seemed in fundamental sync with average people, more so than Coleman and Humphrey: the Minnesota Motorcycle Riders Association Freedom Rally. Trying to build support in one of Minnesota's niche constituencies, Norm Coleman wore a leather jacket and pledged to veto helmet laws (which periodically come up in the legislature). Humphrey sent a letter in lieu of a personal appearance in which he promised that he would not "initiate or support" such legislation. Ventura stole the show, however, showing up in a leather-fringe jacket and waxing poetic about his days in a California motorcycle gang called The Mongols. Nobody could possibly doubt that he would veto helmet laws, and his performance received the longest and loudest applause from the riders assembled.[121]

Compare this instance of the "common touch" to the other two candidates. In a profile of Norm Coleman, listed among his hobbies was squash. If Norm Coleman is not one of the few people in Minnesota who know what squash is, he is surely one of the only ones to actually play it.[122] As for Humphrey, when the *Pioneer Press* ran a feature with the headline "How in Touch with Real Life Are the Candidates for the State's Highest Office?" that consisted of reporting each candidate's responses to a set of questions, he responded to a question about how he takes his coffee by saying that he did not drink much coffee—he drinks herbal tea. Similarly, the same article asked for the candidates' favorite TV show; Coleman's was the evening news ("I can't tell you the last time I watched a sitcom on TV"), Humphrey liked British comedies on public television, and Ventura confessed to loving *The Young and the Restless*. Asked if their children attended public or private school, Ventura said, "Public. Always," while Coleman acknowledged sending his children to the most expensive Catholic grade school in St. Paul, and Humphrey, who spent a good part of the campaign accusing Coleman of trying to destroy public schools by supporting "vouchers" for private school (which he did not), admitted that his own son had attended high school at *the* private high school in the state.[123]

On October 1 the *Pioneer Press* contained a guest editorial by a St. Paul resident named Buzz Cummins, a Republican and former staffer for Governor Al Quie. Cummins began by praising Coleman's record in St. Paul and his leadership. He then wrote that, although he did not support Humphrey out of concern that he might be unable to restrain his urge to spend, he thought he is a good man with a good heart who would be a fine governor. Acknowledging that despite what each would have voters believe, Minnesota had two fine men from whom to select a governor, he added, "And yet I am feeling an almost irresistible urge to vote for an unqualified former wrestler for governor." He explained this with a reference to the nasty tone the Coleman-Humphrey race had taken, saying that "attacking Humphrey for a 25-year-old vote on drug penalties when your own candidate has already admitted he actually did inhale is simply stupid. And if the 'Farmer Coleman' ad misrepresenting Norm's views on the family farm weren't so annoying, it would simply be pathetic."[124] He further lamented "the immediate instinct of the professional campaign handlers to go negative by demeaning and demonizing their opponents [that] serves only to discredit any already damaged political system." He closed with an image of "Governor Jesse putting a figure-four leg lock on the speaker of the house," an image that to him seemed somehow more innocuous than the bitterness of the conventional political landscape.

As proof that the meanness of the race was noticed, the September 23 *Star Tribune* ran a story on the negative ads being run by both the DFL and GOP camps. It discussed the confusion over the cease-fire in negative ads after Mrs. Humphrey's death and featured officials from both campaigns hurling accusations of everything from bad faith to lying. It also discussed the most recent addition to the DFL arsenal, which was perhaps the most negative of the whole campaign, an ad featuring a picture of Coleman with the words "slippery," "false," and "a bucket of mud."[125]

The Debate Season

Jesse Ventura was invited to all six of the televised statewide debates, and the overwhelming consensus of observers was that he won them all; one reporter said that he "creamed" Humphrey and Coleman.[126] Kathy Czar conceded victory to Ventura, but with a dimmer view. She studied acting in college and said of Ventura's performance, "During the debates, it was very clear that he was a professional media personality. He was very good with nonverbal body language. Not a lot of content."[127] There is no doubt that his stage presence was positive.[128] Regardless of how much content he brought to bear (everyone has a different opinion on this), the debates were the moment when his candidacy began to catch fire.

Dick Dietz, Reform Party vice-chair, recalled, "I can remember talking to my father, a lifelong Democrat, on the phone during a debate on TV, and we sort of watched it over the phone. I said, 'Look at this guy compared to these politicians.' And my dad said, 'Yeah, but he's a wrestler. And I said 'Listen to his answers.' And my dad said, 'Oh, okay, that makes sense.'"[129]

The Coleman campaign's strategy was to avoid confronting Ventura, to instead woo his supporters by appealing to their issues. Thus, during the first debate, he said, "Jesse, you've raised the right point."[130] Humphrey made similar goodwill overtures to Ventura supporters; when Ventura said that rebating farm taxes after the fact would not help farmers during the coming year to buy things like seed, he began his response by saying, "Jesse is actually right on that."[131]

During the debate, Ventura was at times short on details (though none were requested) and instead peppered his discussion with phrases like "With freedom comes responsibility, but I prefer freedom and I think people will show the responsibility." But on other issues, he was able to steer the debate and came across as well-informed. Humphrey and Coleman seemed to say the same things over and over—Coleman reminding people that he had a record of cutting spending and taxes, Skip reminding people that he was the only one to present a budget plan. Taxes and tax cuts were the controlling theme of the debate, and throughout it Ventura seemed a sincere antipolitician with more common sense than anyone else running. He spoke passionately and genuinely on the budget surplus:

> I'm the only candidate that stood at the steps of the capitol during the $4 billion surplus and said "Give it back." That was easy money to give back. It was unbudgeted, there it was. It could have gone back to the people. Instead, where were these two during that time? Nowhere. Now they're talking tax cuts. I think it may be because November 3rd is coming up.[132]

He also managed to deflect any nascent concern about his general lack of specifics for governing, saying, "They're both making promises on their expected surpluses and all that. I'm not going to make promises I can't keep."

On education, he avoided staking out a position beyond calling open enrollment "touchy feely, good-time policy" and pointed to his own well-chosen running mate "that unfortunately can't join me at all these functions, you know why? She's there, Mae Schunk, teaching in the classroom right as we speak, if we back up five hours today."[133] He also seemed extremely sincere when he railed on the wastefulness of government:

I want to get in there and get my hands in there to find out where that pork is. Because we've discovered right now, speaking of education, there's $281 million by law that's supposed to be allocated for smaller class sizes. It's not being done. It's being shipped out, it's being spent on other things.[134]

It is difficult to convey how much better Ventura seemed to perform than Humphrey and Coleman. Many observers noted that he seemed full of common sense, much better able to fix problems that could be fixed and leave alone those that could not. Reporter Eric Escala was at the debate and said of Ventura, "He was clearly the winner. Afterward, at the receptions, people congratulated him and kept wanting to touch him. I knew then that he'd be a factor."[135]

Norm Coleman and Skip Humphrey held alternating news conferences on October 5. Humphrey started the day by accusing Norm Coleman of supporting, and operating a stealth campaign for, vouchers for private-school tuitions. "Norm Coleman has tried to hide his support for vouchers," he said, claiming that Coleman would siphon money away from public schools. "Just ask Norm if he supports vouchers," he suggested. Coleman shot back later in the day and accused Humphrey of deceiving voters; Coleman reiterated that he supported education tax credits for lower-income families, not vouchers, and that these tax credits could be used for computers, education camps, and tutors. Coleman hoped to extend the eligibility for the $2,000 credits from a $33,500 income to $40,000; he retorted, "Skip, tell us whether you support education credits." Humphrey, who seemed at times chronically unable to address an issue without equivocation, told reporters that he did not "necessarily" support them, suggesting that it was important to find out whether the program is meeting its goals. Humphrey soon renewed his attacks against Coleman on farm issues both on TV and on radio, surreptitiously referencing Coleman's a-little-too-slick New Yorker image.[136]

At a debate on October 5, Humphrey and Coleman slugged it out over merit pay for teachers. Coleman made his case over and over for merit pay and stated again that he did not support vouchers. Humphrey again would not say whether he supported merit pay (he was, as a Democrat, beholden to the anti–merit pay teacher unions' support) and continued to accuse Coleman of a voucher plan designed to destroy public schools, which forced Coleman to spell out again the difference between his plan for educational tax credits and vouchers for private schools. The whole mess was wildly confusing, while Ventura sat by, from time to time recalling the importance of neighborhood schools and lamenting the dearth of parent participation in things such as the PTA and, as always, laying out his simple plans for governing without any real challenges from either of the other two.

The Advertisements

Bill Hillsman is chief executive officer of a small advertising firm in Minneapolis, but he is more noted as the well-regarded architect of Paul Wellstone's low-cost ($500,000) 1990 Senate advertising campaign. He created the famous "Fast-paced Paul" ad that had Wellstone speaking at a comically fast rate to highlight his small campaign coffers (compared to those of rival Rudy Boschwitz). But his greater triumph may be that by joining the Ventura campaign he became the person most responsible (other than Ventura) for the result of the election.

Hillsman likes populists. He has a soft spot for anyone who "really represents the population at large, not the two major parties. They monopolize the political system for a small group of people. . . . We don't need a third party so much as we need a second party."[137] Hillsman worked for Doug Johnson in the Democratic primary, who "was the real populist in the race. The unions endorsed Mike Freeman, but we had all these union guys coming up to him and saying, 'Hey, Dougie, I gotta wear this stupid button, but I'm pulling the lever for you.'" In retrospect, says Hillsman, "Nobody was going to beat Humphrey in the primary."

Hillsman first noticed Ventura during the state fair: "Jesse was invited to the candidate forums. It didn't take me long to figure out that Jesse was the second choice for most people. And it doesn't take a political genius to figure out that since all but one of these other guys' supporters would be disappointed, there was going to be a good base there for Jesse to make an independent run."

In September Hillsman contacted Barkley about joining Ventura's campaign. They finally got together during the first week of October. Hillsman was surprised to learn that "there wasn't any real strategy. . . . These guys really didn't have a plan."[138] Hillsman, in contrast, already had in his mind a thorough plan to elect Jesse Ventura governor of Minnesota.

The demographic of a potential Ventura voter was clear to Hillsman: "I thought he had a great appeal to what some people would call Reagan Democrats or blue-collar Democrats—guys who live in the third ring suburb, got a wife and kids, maybe a boat or whatever. These are the guys you have to get." He drew on his experience with the Wellstone campaign, saying, "It's the Wellstone swing vote. . . . It's the real politically independent middle part of the state. There are plenty of these guys, blue-collar guys or whatever, who vote for Wellstone to this day but maybe don't agree with him on a single issue. They pull the lever for him every time because they respect his honesty, they trust him, and they think it's good to have someone like him in Washington."[139]

For his initial strategy meeting with the Ventura campaign, he wrote on a presentation board the archetype of the sort of voter he thought the campaign could sway: "Male 25–54, working class, outdoors, cabin, toys owner [i.e., boats, personal water craft, four-wheelers, motorcycle]."

"I met with Jesse on a Sunday night, and we presented the entire plan for the race."[140] Hillsman does not mince his words; he said, "If you're going to do this, you gotta *do* it. If you're going to run as a pop-ulist, you're only gonna have one shot. The press is never gonna treat you like they do that first time." Both because he knew that the votes Ventura could win were located near the Twin Cities and because the campaign had to start maximizing its time and resources, he immediately constrained Ventura's campaigning to the Twins Cities and suburbs. He recalls, "Before I came on board, Jesse would drive an hour and a half to be on cable news in Mankato. . . . I said, we got thirty days left, the Twin Cities media market covers 80 percent of the state, we're going to keep him here." He also challenged everyone's commitment to the race, telling them that because they were going to definitely be out-spent, they could not be outworked. Hillsman believed the Ventura campaign now had one important advantage, however: "Mostly 'cause they got me on their side, they're not going to get outsmarted."[141]

On October 7 the *Pioneer Press* ran a story on the previous night's debate in the DFL-stronghold Iron Range entitled, "Iron Range Hears Ventura's Siren Song in Debate." The beginning of the story had a teacher from Hibbing saying, "It was something to see a Democrat with a name like Humphrey come up here to Northern Minnesota and probably come in third."[142] It was during this debate that Ventura forgot the name of the Iron Range Resources and Rehabilitation Board, the government-sponsored economic development program for the chronically depressed region. Known as the "I-Triple-R-B" and the lifeblood of the Iron Range, its name should be second nature to anyone who wants to campaign here. Instead, when asked about it, Ventura said, "What is the list of letters again—the I-triple-F?" to surprisingly robust laughter. "I made what every expert would consider the biggest mistake you could make in a debate: be asked a question and simply say 'I don't know,'" Ventura recalled in an interview after the election.[143] Phil Madsen, Ventura's webmaster, remembers the event as an especially positive moment in the campaign: "Jesse was unfamiliar, and he said so, and a whole bunch of support came over because he was being honest. You wouldn't believe the e-mails we had coming in. People were really impressed with his honesty."[144]

The *Star Tribune* on October 7 declared, "Campaign Becomes a Numbers Game." It featured Norm Coleman alleging that Humphrey's proposals would cost $5.6 billion in additional spending in the next biennial budget, the Humphrey campaign accusing Coleman of "taking every speech and every position paper" and distorting it, Humphrey in turn accusing Coleman of setting the state up for "a billion-dollar budget hole" and "tax-cut gimmickry" that would cost the state $2.5 billion to benefit the rich, and Coleman responding in turn with a news conference featuring Governor Carlson chiding Humphrey's spendthrift ways.[145] While the fate of the budget is a fair subject for debate, other questions arise from this exchange: How much did the two major party candidates tear each other down to the benefit of Ventura? How much attention does the average voter give to esoteric number-crunching? Why did the major-party candidates not realize how bad they looked to voters and how good Ventura looked by comparison?

Another example of the pettiness that ran so deep between Coleman and Humphrey came three days later, when Coleman filed an official complaint in all eighty-seven counties under the state's Fair Campaign Practices Act, claiming that Humphrey and his campaign had purposely lied about his position on the family farm (by drawing numerous, tenuous extrapolations of his FarmFest comments).[146] Coleman asked for a grand jury investigation, the Humphrey campaign and the DFL Party protested, and the whole thing more or less faded into the background for the rest of the campaign, the net effect contributing to the perception that Jesse Ventura solely sat above the fray.

On October 11, State Senator Bob Lessard of International Falls, a representative of a more conservative DFL in northern Minnesota, endorsed Coleman over Humphrey.[147] On October 15, the *Pioneer Press* released a poll conducted in conjunction with the NBC affiliate and Minnesota Public Radio. It had a 13-point lead for Humphrey over Coleman, 44 to 31 percent. Ventura came in with 15 points, a 5-point rise since the previous public poll (internal Republican polling had him in the low 20-point range).[148] Ventura, for his part, was uninterested. "The only poll I care about is November 3," he said.[149] In the accompanying article, one of the voters who had converted to Venturaism was quoted saying, "I think he's got as much common sense as any of them, and I think that's all it takes."

The second week in October found the Ventura campaign with "dire cash woes" according to the *Pioneer Press*. The campaign had been unable to find funding for TV commercials. Barkley had appealed to the national party, but Ross Perot and his people had declined to send the $20,000 allowed under state law.[150] Around the same time, the pollster working for the Coleman campaign announced to the inner sanctum of the campaign during a conference call, "You know, Ventura could win this thing."[151] Though at the time those in the campaign were still dismissive of the idea, Chris Georgacas now believes that their pollster saw the campaign through the lens of objective, hard data. Removed from the day-to-day fighting of the campaign, he saw the reality of Ventura's growing appeal.

Governor Carlson urged caution in all things fiscal on October 17, warning the candidates and the state against doling out the surplus with apparent impunity. The same day, Bill Cooper wrote a guest editorial in the *Star Tribune* that pinned the state's increased crime rate on Humphrey, writing:

> In the 16 years under Attorney General Humphrey, drug use (which in 1973 was no big deal) [a reference to Humphrey's previously mentioned vote in the state senate] has become a cancer on our society. The number of reported violent crimes has risen from just under 8,000 to almost 16,000, almost doubling. Under Humphrey murders increased 34 percent, rapes 160 percent, robberies 28 percent and assaults 105 percent. . . . Now candidate Humphrey has a new plan to fight crime in Minnesota. A plan that State Sen. Doug Johnson, DFL-Tower, called a blueprint for the actions the attorney general's office should have taken over the last 16 years.[152]

The *Pioneer Press* formally endorsed Norm Coleman for governor on October 18. The editorial board praised his tax cut package, "reducing Minnesota's inordinately high taxes, putting more money back in taxpayers' pockets and fostering economic growth." Coleman, they said, would also expand choice in education and raise standards, and he would step up the war on crime. Humphrey, the paper claimed, still "seems wedded to the politics of the past" with "one pricey promise after another." As for Ventura, "an entertaining and engaging candidate," they cited his lack of experience and the absence of any other indicator that would suggest he would be able to lead a state with a $2.1 billion biennial budget and more than 30,000 employees.[153]

On October 19, Humphrey called for a special session to provide relief to farmers. "This shouldn't be about politics," he said. "It can't wait until the next governor is sworn in."[154] The same day, Senator Joseph Lieberman of Connecticut was in town, stumping for Humphrey.

However, things were growing dark for Skip Humphrey: A *Star Tribune* poll published on October 20, less than two weeks before the election, put Humphrey and Coleman in a dead heat, 35 percent to 34. Perhaps the most significant result of the poll was that Ventura's support had doubled to 21 percent. *Star Tribune* reporter Bob von Sternberg was with Ventura when he heard the news: "[When] we got the poll results, and I showed him the numbers, his reaction was incredulity and, at the same time, there was this light going on. I don't think he ever thought he could win before that."[155]

Chris Gilbert, a political science professor at Gustavus Adolphus College, said of the poll, "My perception of the debates is that Humphrey has not come across as the leader in the race. The campaign doesn't stand out as a brilliant campaign." Ventura's percentages he called "a remarkable figure for a third-party candidate at any point in the campaign."[156] A *Pioneer Press* article from October 21 declared the race to be finally "on," as Coleman galloped along, momentum on his side. The same day, Jack Kemp came to the Twin Cities to help him campaign. With the tide turning against Humphrey and Ventura clearly stealing his support, Humphrey attacked Ventura for the first time, pointing to his lack of a budget plan. "How's he going to pay for housing? How's he going to invest more in education?" asked Humphrey at an African-American church in St. Paul.

Secretary of Agriculture Dan Glickman came to help Humphrey on October 22, and Bob Dole came to town for Coleman the same day. The Ventura campaign, meanwhile, had yet to air a television ad.

During the third week of October, the Ventura campaign released its first ad—on the radio. Still unable to find the money for television ads, they were relegated to the cheaper medium. Hillsman designed an ad that played off the theme from the movie *Shaft*.[157] It had a male voice singing verses such as

While the other guys were cashing government checks,
he was in the Navy getting dirty and wet.

while in the background women croon, "Oooooh, Jesse." Hillsman wanted to use Ventura's distinctive voice and so had him say between the verses things like "Stop, you're making me blush."[158]

Coleman came as close to an actual attack on Ventura as he ever did when his campaign cut a TV ad in the last week of October that had beneath pictures of the three candidates the words, "Only one candidate will deliver permanent tax cuts. Only one." Then the pictures of Ventura and Humphrey fade into the background, leaving a color picture of Coleman and the words "Cut taxes 5 years in a row."[159]

The next day the *Star Tribune* described the Reform Party campaign as having "catapulted" to "a new level of credibility." The same article had the state senate's only official Independent, Charlie Berg, endorsing Coleman and saying of his west-central Minnesota district, "The one thing I hear most of all is, 'Well, I'm not voting for Humphrey.'"[160] Around this same time a Republican Party official who worked on Coleman's campaign and who saw internal GOP tracking polls told a friend from Washington, "I think we're gonna win, but if we lose, we're going to lose to Jesse."[161]

Part of Hillsman's strategy for Ventura was that he minimize how much he discussed both conspiracies and his support for legalizing drugs and prostitution, but Ventura apparently decided to disregard the latter part of Hillsman's advice on October 21 when he suggested at a business group luncheon that perhaps Minnesota should consider legalizing prostitution. "It's a lot easier to control something when it's legal than when it's illegal. Nevada doesn't seem to have a problem, do they?" he rhetorically queried the diners.[162] He later insisted that he was just giving his personal opinion, not trying to set an agenda. Ventura had to backpedal and defend himself. Saying that the media coverage misrepresented him, he said, "It insinuated that I'm leaving room for legalization. . . . I'm leaving room for studying it." Later, in a radio interview, he was more forceful, saying, "Jesse Ventura is not going to legalize prostitution in any way, shape or form."[163] Of course, Coleman and Humphrey seized on the opportunity to attack their newly legitimate rival, Humphrey saying, "That's not what the people of Minnesota are all about," and Coleman calling it "one of the most absurd and outrageous statements I have heard in the whole campaign."[164] Although insisting that he did not want to legalize prostitution and was simply leaving room for its study, Ventura nevertheless added, "I'll stand by it, and I'm not going to fudge on it."[165]

But on October 26, in an editorial titled "Ventura's Straight Talk Merits Respect" in the *Pioneer Press,* Nick Coleman, one of Minnesota's most respected columnists, came to his defense. He wrote, "Ventura, whose nickname has never been 'The Brain,' committed a cardinal sin in politics: He dared to think out loud. . . . He pillories the boring, unthinking styles of Humphrey and Coleman, who avoid taking stands and avoid acknowledging the ambiguity we all know characterizes real life. . . . We could thank Ventura for his open-mouthed candor and tell him that, while we're not interested in legalized prostitution, we are interested in a candidate for governor who is willing to depart from the prepared scripts, speak his mind and take chances."[166]

Humphrey did not seem to take a similar cue from Ventura's behavior, because just as he had gone after Coleman for flip-flopping on the concealed-carry issue, so did he provide an opportunity for Coleman to accuse him of the same on the issue of gay marriage. In an interview in July, Humphrey had said that he was not opposed to same-sex marriage and that gays and lesbians should be extended the right of civil marriage. Coleman, campaigning in southwestern Minnesota, on October 23 criticized Humphrey as a supporter of gay marriage; Republican legislators held a news conference at the Capitol to do the same thing. Humphrey had to call a news conference to say that he did not in fact support gay marriage, announcing, "Gay marriages are not sanctioned by the state. The people of Minnesota are not going to accept that." Coleman wasted no time in accusing Humphrey of switching his position, saying, "If he's afraid of the truth, that's unfortunate."[167] In fact, there was serious turmoil in the Coleman campaign over how to treat the issue. Their own internal polling showed that support for gay marriage was the issue that could most hurt Humphrey and Ventura. The ad had been created and was ready to be aired, but Coleman made the decision that, though he himself was opposed to the creation of gay marriage by government, he did not want to prey upon homosexuals for political advantage. The ad never aired.[168]

Coleman was slightly more willing to go after Ventura during a debate on October 24. When Ventura did his usual dismissive sniffing about careers in government, Coleman retorted that he was proud of his service as a prosecutor, would make no apologies for being a public servant, and that to belittle their careers so flippantly was an "absurd proposition."[169]

That same day the Ventura campaign aired its first television ad, having finally found a loan to pay for it (discussed in the next chapter). Designed by Hillsman, it began with a red stripe and a white stripe across the screen, "Republicans" written on top over the red stripe and "Democrats" across the bottom over the white. The shot widens out, and the words disappear, revealing the stripes as an extreme close-up on an American flag while this voiceover is spoken:

Usually Minnesotans have two choices in elections: Republicans or Democrats. Which is hardly a choice. Both Norm Coleman and Skip Humphrey take special interest money, they have almost no experience

in the private sector, and both take time off with pay to campaign for
higher office. But this year there's a real alternative: a man who's a
card-carrying union member, a military veteran, and a volunteer football coach. In other words, one of us. Don't waste your vote on politics
as usual. Vote Reform Party candidate Jesse Ventura for Governor.[170]

It might not seem so, but this is a form of an attack ad, one in a different, more subtle form—it attacks politicians and "the system" in general, asserting a dichotomy of "regular people" and "professional politicians" and encouraging a general revolt. It does what Ventura and his
campaign sought to do throughout the campaign: "We wanted them to
look like slick, out-of-the can, trained, professional politicians," Ventura
admitted. "I wanted those two to be painted with the same brush . . .
that, OK, over here you're going to get business as usual, you're going
to get the usual professional politician who has climbed the ranks."[171]
To get to people he felt could be energized by the Ventura campaign,
Hillsman ran the commercials on nontraditional media venues: Minnesota Vikings games, *Saturday Night Live,* FOX-TV sports shows.
"Campaigns for some reason don't [usually] advertise on FOX—it's too
'risky,'" says Hillsman.[172]

The *Star Tribune* endorsed Skip Humphrey on October 25, which
surprised nobody given the paper's tendency toward liberal proselytiz-
ing in its news reporting. The endorsement praised Humphrey's plan for
"targeted" tax cuts that would help address "the income disparity between haves and have-nots that has characterized economic expansion
in this decade."[173] It lauded Humphrey's deftness on education issues
and decried Coleman's "flirtation with vouchers" while disputing the
notion that Humphrey was antibusiness. As for Jesse Ventura, the paper
dismissed him because of his lack of allies in the legislature, conclud-
ing that Humphrey was the best choice as someone who "grasps the
need to invest in people today to have a better tomorrow."[174]

Late October found the Democrat and Republican candidates in the
state's hinterlands, trying to shore up support they should have ce-
mented long before—Coleman in rural farm areas, Humphrey in the
Iron Range.[175] At the same time, the Republicans launched ads in the
Iron Range claiming that Humphrey supported handgun registration and
did not want to put restrictions on partial-birth abortion, only the latter
of which is really true.[176] Meanwhile, Ventura held rallies in the Twin
Cities, one of which was for students at the University of Minnesota.

During this time, interest groups that had attached themselves to
Humphrey and Coleman rolled out ads for their candidates. A teachers'

union, Education Minnesota, produced an ad on behalf of Humphrey that concerned education issues; the Coalition of Minnesota Businesses paid for an attack ad against Humphrey's alleged penchant for policies that hurt business; and a group known as Americans for Job Security launched a sharp attack on Humphrey's fiscal policies.[177] The Humphrey campaign released a new ad that featured a county sheriff praising Humphrey as a tough-on-crime, tough-on-guns candidate and Norm Coleman as someone who wants "to let just about anyone carry a loaded, concealed weapon, anywhere."[178]

The penultimate debate took place on October 27. The recent polls having made such a stir, Coleman and Humphrey were more willing to go head-to-head with Ventura this time. Norm Coleman stuck to his tried-and-true theme of having a record of spending cuts and tax cuts, turning even a question about workers' compensation laws into an awkward segue to tax cuts. Skip Humphrey stuck to his own tried-and-true theme of investing in the future for Minnesota, nebulous answers to questions about "dynamic partnerships," and his being the only candidate to have presented a budget plan. Jesse was again much more exciting to listen to, not just because he was Jesse Ventura and expectations were low, but because he gave interesting and original answers. And despite Coleman's and Humphrey's belated jabs at him, he still managed to parry their blows while sounding the most earnest and sincere of the three.

The format of the first half of the debate allowed the candidates to ask each other questions. When Norm Coleman asked Jesse Ventura a question that gave himself an opportunity to again list his own plan for tax cuts, Ventura responded by thanking Coleman for stealing his idea for a "trigger" law that would automatically return any future surpluses as tax cuts.[179] The question from Humphrey was supposed to be about education tax credits for higher education but was anteceded with a mention of Ventura's alleged support for legalizing drugs and prostitution. Stealing his thunder, Ventura responded, "I stated unequivocally that I did not support the legalization of prostitution and drugs. That was my original answer to the question, but the press conveniently left that out and I guess you followed along."[180] This is not really true, of course, but Humphrey's thunder was gone. When Ventura got his turn, he accused Coleman of actually raising property taxes in St. Paul, which did not seem to stick very well, but when he turned his gaze to Humphrey, he said:

> You like to claim that you're the education governor, that's what you want to be. And yet a week ago we had a debate scheduled for over

100 high school students at Mall of America that had been scheduled
for quite some time. In fact a young lady in Hibbing told me how
thrilled she was to be able to come down and participate in that debate. I would like to ask why you pulled out of that debate as well as
others, and why you would choose that one to pull out of; to the best
of my knowledge, correct me if I'm wrong, you attended the Vikings
game that day instead of the debate.[181]

Humphrey, perhaps without thinking, began his response by saying, "I
did have a scheduled appointment at the Vikings game, no doubt about
that." Ventura's ability to evoke a response from the audience was notable. Since the audience was not allowed to clap, the next best way to
gauge response was laughter. Ventura got a laugh six times. The only
other laugh came when one of the moderators prefaced a question by re-
capping Coleman's changed worldview, from being a roadie for a rock
band in his youth and endorsing Paul Wellstone for Senate to becoming
the favorite son of the Republican Party of Minnesota. The laughs came
with the question "Who are you?" And, true to form, Coleman retreated
to his standard answer about governing as a conservative by cutting
taxes and spending, that he got older and paid taxes, had kids, understood money better, and so on. But here is what he did not do: He did
not take the opportunity to stop the questioner and say, Look, I switched
parties because I was growing uncomfortable with the rigidity of the
Democratic Party, which apparently believes in diversity of everything
except thought, especially since I was always pro-life and against high
taxes, and then, over time, I had come to see that the best way to be
compassionate, which was why I had been a Democrat in the first place,
was to help people help themselves. But he didn't do that; he didn't
squash remaining doubts about his sincerity, didn't offer a reasonable
explanation—instead he retreated to his same campaign pitch in a season where voters were looking for people of integrity and intellectual
honesty to lead them.

One moderator did go after Ventura aggressively about the legalization of drugs, mentioning Ventura's *High Times* interview during the
summer in which he said that the government should "tax the hell" out
of marijuana and then lower *his* taxes. Ventura responded by saying that
he was in favor of industrial hemp and medicinal marijuana. The moderator pressed him, and Ventura responded by saying that his point was
only that it made no sense to treat as criminals those who "inflict stu-
pidity on themselves."[182] The moderator accused him of "hedging."
Ventura insisted he was not, that he did not want to legalize drugs, and
that he would not try to do so as governor.

In their closing statements, Coleman and Humphrey iterated their themes and pledges yet again. Ventura decided to spend his allotted time encouraging people to vote, saying that they owed it to the veterans who had fought for their right to do so, that it was their civic duty. He finished with a plea for people to believe that a vote for Jesse Ventura was not a wasted vote, and he gave everyone something to think about by asserting that if such fears had carried weight a century and a half ago, then "Abraham Lincoln would not have been president of the United States."[183]

Around this time Hillsman made and released a new TV ad, which he again aired during shows like *The Simpsons* and *Saturday Night Live*. It featured two young boys playing outside with action figures, one of whom was a Ken™ doll whose head was replaced with a more Ventura-ish bald one. As the excited children run up to the action figures, the dialogue begins: "New! From the Reform Party! It's the new Jesse Ventura Action Figure! You can make Jesse battle special interest groups!" The boy holding "Ventura" then says, "I don't want your stupid money!" The narrator cuts in, "And party politics!" The boy holding a second, non-Ventura doll says, "We politicians have powers the average citizen can't comprehend!" The narrator continues, "You can also make Jesse lower taxes, improve public education, and fight for the things Minnesotans really care about." The boy holding Ventura says, "This bill wastes taxpayer money. Redraft it!" and the narrator concludes, "Don't waste your vote on politics as usual. Vote Reform Party Candidate Jesse Ventura for governor!"[184] Usual, boring political advertising this was not, and Hillsman explained its success: "The action figure ad was probably the riskiest political ad ever run by anyone. But here was a candidate who understood popular culture. It took him two and a half seconds to decide to do it."[185]

On October 28, *Pioneer Press* columnist Joe Soucheray predicted that Minnesota "could be looking at four years of Gov. Turnbuckle." He then enumerated Jesse's qualities, saying that he is, in theory, "everything we want in a politician." He explained his reasoning:

He is an open and candid family man, skeleton-free, who intends to set aside his personal life, travel to the state house to serve and then return to his private pursuits. He is so incapable of deception that he said something the other day about legalizing prostitution. Never mind that such legislation would never even get to his desk, no politician in his right mind would even go down that road. But then, Jesse is no politician.[186]

He continued, "Of the three candidates, Ventura is the one who was educated in Minnesota public schools, served in the active military, works
in the private sector and worked the State Fair by himself. He has no
people." He concludes with an unusual but eloquent endorsement of
Ventura:

> There is something else Ventura has going for him, something that we
> don't ever even let ourselves think about when it comes to politics. He
> would be fun. Yes, this is particularly true for me, or any ink-stained
> wretch: four years of writing about Gov. Turnbuckle. But fun nonethe-
> less. With Jesse we'd not only get our money back, but living in the
> mansion on Summit we would have a Jetski-riding, lake cabin–own-
> ing, suburban home owner with a Harley and a bald head who would
> so terrorize the careerists with his blunt assessments of their useless-
> ness that he might drive them away, or crazy.[187]

The *Pioneer Press,* which had endorsed Coleman, ran a staff editorial
the very next day about Ventura's popularity, calling him a "wake-up
call" to the major parties and their "single-issue factions."[188]

All three candidates were barnstorming throughout the last few
days of the campaign. Ventura held a student rally at the University of
Minnesota, after which four of five students interviewed by the *Pioneer
Press* planned to vote for him. "What really struck me is how he is really fighting for the people," said one. "He seems to be a guy you could
just go up to and pat on the back and say, 'What's going on?'" Said another: "He has a few positions I don't agree with, but I think he's a very
honest person."[189] As things rolled along in the other campaigns, the legitimacy of Ventura and the real threat he presented was clear as the attacks came. "A guy like Jesse Ventura gets cute sound bites, but you've
got to ask what his philosophy is," said Skip Humphrey during a stop in
Duluth. DFL allies blasted Ventura for allegedly favoring eliminating
the prevailing wage law on government construction projects.[190] As the
campaign reached its pitch, Secretary of State Joan Growe predicted a
turnout of 53 percent, or just fewer than 1.83 million voters, saying, "It
appears to me that interest in the governor's race is increasing steadily
as we approach election day."

The Drive to Victory

On the Friday before the election, the Ventura campaign began its 72-
hour Drive to Victory in three rented recreational vehicles. Hillsman

conceived of a late-race travel push of some kind as a way of keeping momentum and media attention. "Frankly, I got the idea from Bob Dole [who did similar nonstop travel in 1996]. . . . It worked for a guy like Jesse, you know, big and full of testosterone, an ex-military guy. It was the perfect thing for momentum and to keep us going in the polls right before the election."[191]

They based the route on the targeting data that Hillsman got from Ed Gross. It circled the Twin Cities outer-ring suburbs, with thirty-four stops and major rallies in five cities.[192] On the days leading up to it, Hillsman created a new commercial for the event. It began with a shot of an RV, and an announcer proclaimed excitedly, "Presenting the latest accessory for the Jesse Ventura Action Figure! It's the Victory RV! A full-sized RV that Jesse rides on his 72-hour drive to victory." The shot then cuts to the Jesse Ventura Action Figure from the previous commercial sitting behind the steering wheel of a full-sized RV. The narrator continues, "You too can join the Drive to Victory. Check our website at www.jesseventura.org to find out how. The Jesse Ventura Friday to Monday 72-hour drive to victory. Join in to meet the man, the action figure, and our next governor."[193]

When the Drive to Victory began, Bob von Sternberg, the *Star Tribune* reporter who had been covering Ventura since the summer, remembers that "all of a sudden I wasn't the only one covering him anymore."[194] The Drive to Victory went through Anoka, up to Hibbing, then back west, circling the Twin Cities, through Mankato, and back down to Rochester.

The whole routine was choreographed almost brilliantly. By making the Drive to Victory the subject of the third TV commercial, the campaign let people find out when Ventura would be in their town by getting on the campaign website. Throughout the drive, the website was updated with pictures from earlier stops and information on when the tour would be in which town. ("We all had enormous cell phone bills," remembers Tony Carlson about being part of the so-called "Geek Squad."[195]) During the jaunt between cities, supporters would drive along in the caravan with the RVs, and Ventura would give interviews to local radio stations over a cellular phone. The local news media was alerted in each city, and when Ventura rolled into town, there would be supporters and free press waiting.[196]

Major Twin Cities TV news stations covered the events as well. One story on Ventura's rally at a stop showed a man waiting to greet Ventura, holding a sign that said "MY VOTE COUNTS."[197] The same story featured teenage girls, apparently dressed up for some sort of local pageant; asked why they like Jesse Ventura, one girl responds, "'Cause he stands up for what he believes in no matter what people say."[198]

On October 31, in the midst of the Drive to Victory, Hillary Clinton visited the Humphrey campaign in Minneapolis, praising his leadership and commitment to children's issues.[199] She also described Ventura's campaign as a "carnival sideshow" and discouraged people from paying attention to him. Informed of her comments during a stop in Rochester, Ventura retorted, "It seems to me, rather than being concerned about Minnesota politics, Hillary should be more concerned about leaving Bill home alone."[200]

The second day of the Drive to Victory had the *Pioneer Press* asking whether, if elected, Ventura could govern effectively. Not only was asking this question a ringing salute to his legitimacy as a candidate, but it also ended up answering the question in the affirmative, with one veteran legislator saying, "Working with government is like cage wrestling anyhow." Senator Charlie Berg, who had endorsed Coleman, said that Ventura's fiscal conservatism would allow him to find allies among the Republicans. Gene Merriam, former DFL state senator and Humphrey backer, concurred: "The governor certainly communicates to the public, and the Legislature responds to the public." Even Governor Carlson, a staunch backer of the Republican ticket, said that he too believed Ventura could form practical coalitions with Republican and DFL legislators.

On November 1, as Ventura made stops in his Victory RV, the *Pioneer Press* published a new poll that had him at 27 percent and Humphrey and Coleman at 32 percent each, making the race a statistical dead heat.[201] Worried about Ventura's macho image and how it might affect female voters, Hillsman aired one last television advertisement that has come to be known as the "Jesse the Mind" ad. Shot in black and white, it begins with Ventura (actually, a body double) sitting on a block in the middle of a room, as Rodin's *The Thinker*. The words "The Body" flash on the screen. The camera shot is close to him, rotating around his muscular frame, catching shadows, as an aria plays in the background. Next, "The Mind" flashes. As the camera rotates and the fat lady sings, the dialogue is gently spoken:

> Navy Seal. Union member. Volunteer high school football coach. Outdoorsman. Husband of 23 years. Father of two. A man who will fight to return Minnesota's budget surplus to the taxpayers. Who will fight to lower property and income taxes. Who does not accept money from special interest groups. And who will work to improve public education by lowering class sizes.

The commercial ends with a direct shot of Ventura's face. He looks into the camera, smirks ever-so-slightly, and winks.[202] A lot of people in the Ventura campaign did not want to air the "Jesse the Mind" commercial, mostly because they feared viewers might think he was naked (even after they airbrushed the shorts, making them very obvious in the shot). Hillsman, always sure of himself, disagreed: "I said that we gotta do it because there's a lot of stuff people don't know about Jesse Ventura, like that he's been married twenty-three years or that he has two kids, that he's a family guy. I thought there's a lot of female voters we could get."[203]

After the ad aired, Humphrey and Coleman barnstormed the state to light a fire under the party faithful. In the end, their efforts did not matter.

The Mind Triumphant

Election day in Minnesota had some of the nicest November weather in recent memory—sunny and warm—and this probably contributed to the 61 percent voter turnout. Many of those interviewed described overflowing polling stations and lines longer than they had seen in any other election. Some precincts had turnout as high as 80 percent and ran out of ballots. One precinct had so many voters that its counting machines broke.[204] Many of those interviewed described an "electric" feeling in the air at the polling stations.

It was not until the returns started to come in, though, that people really began to suspect that something dramatic was going on. Ventura was ahead the whole night. Eventually there was more fear in the Republican and Democrat camps about coming in third than about losing the election. Ventura himself was probably one of the last people to accept the reality of the situation. Coleman conceded defeat at 12:45 a.m., saying, "I will work with Jesse Ventura to move this state forward." Humphrey conceded a few minutes later, announcing that he had spoken to Ventura and wished him well. He then said, "The people have spoken, and we have to believe and trust the people."[205]

When it sank in that he had been elected governor of the state, Ventura said that he was still going to keep his promise to do his radio show the next morning. Governor Carlson had made an offer prior to the election to sit down with the winner, and Hillsman suggested that snubbing the governor to do a radio show that could be postponed until later in the day might not be the best way to start his career as governor-elect.

Meanwhile, Tom Brokaw and Maria Shriver were waiting to talk to him. It was time to go out into the bright lights and present to the world the next governor of Minnesota.

Notes

1. Steven Schier, "Jesse's Victory: It Was No Fluke," *Washington Monthly* 31, 1 (January 1999), p. 2. Available on the Internet at http://www.washington-monthly.com/features/1999/9901.schier.ventura.html.

2. Schier, "Jesse's Victory: It Was No Fluke," p. 2.

3. Dick Senese, former DFL chair, 28 July 1999, telephone interview by the author, Cambridge, MA, to Northfield, MN.

4. Kathy Czar, former DFL Party executive director, 19 February 2000, e-mail note to the author.

5. Ibid.

6. This was the case both in 1998 (as will be discussed) and in 2000 when the party endorsed State Senator Jerry Janezich from Chisholm (in the Iron Range), a pretty much regular guy of the old-fashioned DFL quasisocialist type and who owned a bar—and wouldn't it be like Minnesota to send a bar owner to the U.S. Senate? But he was defeated by the steam-rolling money machine of department store heir Mark Dayton, and, depending on how you look at things, this may be indicative of Minnesota's decline in quality of governance.

7. Chris Georgacas, former chairman of the Republican Party of Minnesota and Coleman campaign manager, 4 August 1999, interview by the author, Maplewood, MN.

8. Dane Smith and Kevin Duschshere, "Republicans Announce Plans to Draft Coleman," Minneapolis *Star Tribune*, 6 November 1997, p. 1A.

9. Doug Grow, "Coleman's Next Step: Candidacy for Governor?" Minneapolis *Star Tribune*, 5 November 1997, p. 2B.

10. Chris Georgacas interview, 4 August 1999.

11. Robert Whereatt, "Coleman, Humphrey Off to Quick Starts," Minneapolis *Star Tribune*, 1 March 1998, p. 1A.

12. Ibid.

13. Dane Smith, "It's Official: Coleman Joins the Crowd," Minneapolis *Star Tribune*, 16 February 1998, p. 1B.

14. Ibid.

15. Dennis J. McGrath, "State Sen. Terwilliger Leaves GOP Gubernatorial Race," Minneapolis *Star Tribune*, 25 February 1998, p. 2B.

16. Bill Cooper, chair of the Minnesota Republican Party, 3 September 1999, interview by the author, Wayzata, MN.

17. Jack Meeks, Republican National Committeeman from Minnesota, 17 August 1999, telephone interview by the author, Mahtomedi, MN, to St. Paul, MN.

18. Bill Cooper interview, 3 September 1999.

19. Ibid.

20. Chris Georgacas interview, 4 August 1999.

21. Kathy Czar, former DFL executive director, 21 July 1999, telephone interview by the author, Cambridge, MA, to Minneapolis, MN.

22. Jann Olsten, Coleman campaign adviser, 25 August 1999, telephone interview by the author, Mahtomedi, MN, to St. Paul, MN.

23. Mary McEvoy, former associate chair of the DFL and Freeman campaign outreach director, 22 July 1999, telephone interview by the author, Cambridge, MA, to Minneapolis, MN.

24. Patricia Lopez-Baden, "Ad Watch: Campaign '98," Minneapolis *Star Tribune*, 25 July 1998, p. 3B.

25. Arne Carlson, outgoing Republican governor, 9 September 1999, interview by the author, Minneapolis, MN.

26. Bill Cooper interview, 3 September 1999.

27. Jim Ragsdale, "And the Winners Are. . . . " *St. Paul Pioneer Press*, 20 September 1998, p. 3C.

28. KSTP-TV, St. Paul, "Mark Dayton Profile," aired 11 September 1998. Videocassette of newscast given to author by KSTP-TV.

29. KSTP-TV, St. Paul, "Doug Johnson Profile," aired 10 September 1998. Videocassette of newscast given to author by KSTP-TV.

30. Bill Hillsman, CEO of North Woods Advertising and Ventura campaign political and media consultant, 26 August 1999, interview by the author, Minneapolis, MN.

31. Ted Mondale, DFL candidate for governor and current chair of the Metropolitan Council, 30 August 1999, interview by the author, St. Paul, MN.

32. Robert Whereatt, Dane Smith, and Conrad deFiebre, "Inside Talk," Minneapolis *Star Tribune*, 23 March 1998, p. 3B.

33. Mike Freeman, endorsed DFL candidate for governor, 27 August 1999, interview by the author, Minneapolis, MN.

34. Mike Freeman interview, 27 August 1999.

35. Kathy Czar, 19 February 2000 (e-mail note to the author).

36. Dick Senese interview, 28 July 1999.

37. Mary McEvoy interview, 22 July 1999.

38. Dick Senese interview, 28 July 1999.

39. Mike Freeman interview, 27 August 1999.

40. Ted Mondale interview, 30 August 1999.

41. Kathy Czar interview, 21 July 1999.

42. Mike Freeman interview, 27 August 1999.

43. Ibid.

44. Patricia Lopez-Baden, "Ad Watch: Freeman's TV Debut Is Short on Specifics, Subtle on Attacks," Minneapolis *Star Tribune*, 27 August 1998, p. 9B.

45. Robert Whereatt et al., "Humphrey Leads Pack," Minneapolis *Star Tribune*, 4 June 1998, p. 1A.

46. Hubert Humphrey III, 12 August 1999, interview by the author, Bloomington, MN.

47. Steven Dornfield, "Humphrey: An Old-fashioned Liberal Who Believes in Government," *St. Paul Pioneer Press*, 27 August 1998, p. 16A.

48. Ibid.

49. Robert Whereatt et al., "Humphrey Leads Pack," p. 1A.

50. Bill Hillsman interview, 26 August 1999.

51. Phil Madsen, Ventura campaign webmaster, 2 September 1999, interview by the author, St. Paul, MN.

52. Dean Barkley, chairman of the Minnesota Planning Commission and Ventura campaign manager, 3 August 1999, interview by the author, St. Paul, MN.

53. Ibid.

54. Ibid.

55. Ibid.

56. Phil Madsen interview, 2 September 1999; Dean Barkley interview, 3 August 1999.

57. Doug Friedline, Ventura campaign manager, 1 September 1999, interview by the author, St. Paul, MN

58. Dean Barkley interview, 3 August 1999.

59. As will be discussed in Chapter 3, there is some controversy surrounding whether Ventura was in fact a member of the SEALS.

60. Dane Smith, "Ventura Joins the Fray Race to Follow Carlson," Minneapolis *Star Tribune,* 27 January 1998, p. 1B.

61. Dean Barkley interview, 3 August 1999.

62. Phil Madsen interview, 2 September 1999.

63. Ibid.

64. Dane Smith, "In the Gubernatorial Fund-raising Race, Dayton, Benson Lead Crowded Packs," Minneapolis *Star Tribune,* 3 February 1998, p. 1A.

65. Governor Jesse Ventura, 6 October 1999, discussion with the author, Cambridge, MA.

66. Minnesota Reform Party, "We Shocked the World," 1999. Videocassette purchased from the Minnesota Reform Party.

67. "By the Way . . . ," Minneapolis *Star Tribune,* 26 July 1998, p. 5B.

68. This and the following quotations are from "Candidate Quiz," Minneapolis *Star Tribune,* 27 July 1998, p. 3B.

69. And it is worth noting that this is not just Ventura's libertarian streak; it's pretty easy to find an economist who thinks the idea of taxing people for working is nonsense, and so Ventura does have a degree of sophistication in some areas of how he perceives public policy.

70. "Candidate Quiz," Minneapolis *Star Tribune,* 27 July 1998, p. 3B.

71. Bob von Sternberg, "Ventura Seeks Disillusioned Voters He Needs," Minneapolis *Star Tribune,* 28 July 1998, p. 1B.

72. Dane Smith, "Coleman Under Fire for Gun Position," Minneapolis *Star Tribune,* 14 August 1998, p. 1A.

73. Ibid.

74. Chris Georgacas interview, 4 August 1999.

75. Tom Gillaspy, Minnesota state demographer, 21 June 2000, telephone conversation with the author, Cambridge, MA, to St. Paul, MN.

76. Bill Wareham, "Coleman Says Humphrey Ads Lied About His Farm Comments," AP Wire Service, 10 October 1998, Dateline: St. Paul.

77. Conversation with Tom Gillaspy, 21 June 2000.

78. Mavis Huddle, Ventura campaign secretary, 28 July 1999, telephone interview by the author, Cambridge, MA, to Northfield, MN.

79. DFL Party, "Farmer Ad." Obtained from KTCA-TV, Minneapolis. Available on the Internet at http://www.ktca.org/election98/adwatch.html.

80. Patricia Lopez-Baden, "Ad Watch: Campaign '98," Minneapolis *Star Tribune,* 19 August 1998, p. 3B.

81. Conversation with Tom Gillaspy, 21 June 2000.

82. The math works out to nearly 34.8 percent.

83. Phil Madsen, 25 February 2000, *Re: Quick Questions* (e-mail note to the author).

84. KSTP-TV, St. Paul, "Jesse Ventura Profile." Aired 13 September 1998. Videocassette of newscast given to author by KSTP-TV.

85. KSTP-TV, St. Paul, "How We Got Here." Aired 4 November 1998. Videocassette of newscast given to author by KSTP-TV.

86. Ibid.

87. That someone who is a libertarian in so many ways advocates public funding for a rail system shows the remarkable sophistication, or the nuance, of Ventura's political beliefs.

88. Minnesota Reform Party, "We Shocked the World."

89. Ted Mondale interview, 30 August 1999.

90. Dane Smith, 19 July 1999, telephone interview by the author, Cambridge, MA, to Minneapolis, MN.

91. Minnesota Reform Party, "We Shocked the World."

92. KSTP-TV, St. Paul, "Jesse Ventura Profile."

93. Jesse Ventura, *I Ain't Got Time to Bleed* (New York: Villard Books, 1999), p. 160.

94. Jim Ragsdale, "Classic Tax Fight Takes Shape in Campaign." *St. Paul Pioneer Press,* 2 October 1998, p. 1A.

95. Jim Ragsdale, "Political Candidates Eagerly Weigh In on Strike," *St. Paul Pioneer Press,* 4 September 1998, p. 1A.

96. Jim Ragsdale, "Contenders Labor for Votes Across State," *St. Paul Pioneer Press,* 8 September 1998, p. 1C.

97. Jack Coffman, "Getting on the DFL Bus," *St. Paul Pioneer Press,* 13 September 1998, p. 1C.

98. Mike Freeman interview, 27 August 1999.

99. Patrick Sweeney, "Primary Is About Meeting Citizen's Role, Many Say," *St. Paul Pioneer Press,* 16 September 1998, p. 1A.

100. Ted Mondale interview, 30 August 1999.

101. Mike Freeman interview, 27 August 1999.

102. Jim Ragsdale, "On Their Mark, Get Set, Go," *St. Paul Pioneer Press,* 17 September 1998, p. 1A.

103. Jack B. Coffman, "On Their Mark, Get Set, Go," *St. Paul Pioneer Press,* 17 September 1998, p. 1A.

104. Dave Beal, "Business Fears Humphrey Victory," *St. Paul Pioneer Press,* 20 September 1998, p. 1D.

105. Ibid.

106. Patricia Lopez-Baden, "Coleman Details Tax-Cut Proposal," Minneapolis *Star Tribune,* 18 September 1998, p. 1B.

107. Patrick Sweeney, "Coleman: After an Easy Primary Season, GOP Nominee Has to Get Down to Business," *St. Paul Pioneer Press,* 16 September 1998, p. 8A.

108. Tom Powers, "Election May Hinge on Stadium Issue," *St. Paul Pioneer Press,* 18 September 1998, p. 1C.

109. Jim Ragsdale, "Humphrey Says Debates Must Include Ventura," *St. Paul Pioneer Press,* 19 September 1998, p. 1A.

110. Dick Senese interview, 28 July 1999.

111. "Minnesota Race for Governor: Details, Stark Contrasts Might Lure Voters Back," *St. Paul Pioneer Press,* 17 September 1998, p. 12A.

112. Jim Ragsdale, "GOP Lashed for Running Ads After Brown Death," *St. Paul Pioneer Press,* 23 September 1998, p. 1B.

113. Nick Coleman, "Mourners Remember Minnesota's 'Wonderful Lady,'" *St. Paul Pioneer Press,* 25 September 1998, p. 1A.

114. Robert Whereatt, "Poll Indicates Humphrey Has Strong Lead over Coleman," Minneapolis *Star Tribune,* 23 September 1998, p. 1A.

115. Thomas J. Collins, "Humphrey, Coleman Wary of 'Everyman' Ventura," *St. Paul Pioneer Press,* 24 September 1998, p. 1A.

116. Ibid.

117. Patricia Lopez-Baden, "Ad Watch: Campaign '98," Minneapolis *Star Tribune,* 26 September 1998, p. 3B.

118. Jack B. Coffman, "Coleman, Humphrey Exchange Accusations," *St. Paul Pioneer Press,* 28 September 1998, p. 1E.

119. Jack B. Coffman, "Carlson Stumps on Behalf of Coleman," *St. Paul Pioneer Press,* 29 September 1998, p. 3C.

120. "Ventura Pushes for Smaller Classes in Elementary School," Minneapolis *Star Tribune,* 22 September 1998, p. 3B.

121. "Gubernatorial Candidates Oppose Mandatory Helmets for Motorcyclists," AP Wire Service, 5 October 1998.

122. "The November Lineup," Minneapolis *Star Tribune,* 20 September 1998, p. 4A.

123. "How in Touch with Real Life Are the Candidates for the State's Highest Office? We Asked Them Some Everyday Questions, and Here's What They Had to Say," *St. Paul Pioneer Press* Special Section, "Your Primary Choice Voter's Guide," 3 September 1998, p. 9M.

124. Carl Cummins, "Two Negatives May Equal Positive for Ventura," *St. Paul Pioneer Press,* 1 October 1998, p. 17A.

125. Patricia Lopez-Baden, "Republicans, DFLers Trade Negative Ads and Negative Words," Minneapolis *Star Tribune,* 23 September 1998, 1A.

126. Bob von Sternberg, reporter for the Minneapolis *Star-Tribune,* 18 July 1999, telephone interview by the author, Cambridge, MA, to Minneapolis, MN.

127. Kathy Czar interview, 21 July 1999.

128. When asked what single advantage he had over his opponents going into the race, Governor Ventura said, "My physical size" (Jesse Ventura, 6 October 1999, discussion with the author, Cambridge, MA). Both his opponents were visibly smaller men, and perhaps part of why Ventura did so well in the debates can be explained by viewers' psychological reaction to a candidate's physical presence; but Ventura's ability to command attention is also bound up in his natural charisma, and one should also consider his unusual debating style as a possible advantage.

129. Dick Dietz, vice-chair of the Minnesota Reform Party, 28 July 1999, telephone interview by the author, Cambridge, MA, to Mankota, MN.

130. KTCA-TV, Minneapolis, "October Second Debate." Video recording of the 30 October 1998 debate sponsored by KTCA-TV. Available on the Internet at http://www.ktca.org/election98/debates.html.

131. Ibid.

132. Ibid.

133. Ibid.

134. Ibid.

135. Eric Escala, WCCO (CBS affiliate) political reporter, 26 July 1999, telephone interview by the author, Cambridge, MA, to Minneapolis, MN.

136. Patricia Lopez-Baden, "Ad Watch: Campaign '98," Minneapolis *Star Tribune*, 4 October 1998, p. 3B.

137. This and following quotes from Bill Hillsman interview, 26 August 1999.

138. Ibid.

139. Ibid.

140. Ibid.

141. Ibid.

142. Patrick Sweeney, "Iron Range Hears Ventura's Siren Song in Debate," *St. Paul Pioneer Press*, 7 October 1998, p. 13A.

143. Corey Kiefer, "Citizen Jesse," 1999. Videocassette produced by Red, White, and Blue Brand Productions. Officially licensed merchandise of Ventura for Minnesota, Inc. Purchased by the author.

144. Phil Madsen interview, 2 September 1999.

145. Dane Smith, "Campaign Becomes a Numbers Game," Minneapolis *Star Tribune*, 7 October 1998, p. 4B.

146. Patricia Lopez-Baden, "Coleman Files Complaint Against DFL," *St. Paul Pioneer Press*, 10 October 1998, p. 1B.

147. Robert Whereatt, "DFL Sen. Bob Lessard Backs Coleman," Minneapolis *Star Tribune*, 12 October 1998, p. 5B.

148. Jim Ragsdale, "Poll: Humphrey Tops, Schools Key Issue," *St. Paul Pioneer Press*, 15 October 1998, p. 1A.

149. Ibid.

150. "Barkley: Ventura Campaign Has Dire Cash Woes," *St. Paul Pioneer Press*, 9 October 1998, p. 7C.

151. Chris Georgacas interview, 4 August 1999.

152. Bill Cooper, "Humphrey Shares Blame for State's Increase in Crime," Minneapolis *Star Tribune*, 17 October 1998, p. 23A.

153. "Our Choice for Governor: Coleman Will Lead Us to a Brighter Future," *St. Paul Pioneer Press*, 18 October 1998, p. 16A.

154. Jim Ragsdale, "Humphrey Wants Special Session on Tax Relief for Farmers," *St. Paul Pioneer Press*, 20 October 1998, p. 2B.

155. Bob von Sternberg interview, 18 July 1999.

156. Robert Whereatt, "Suddenly, It's a Dead Heat," Minneapolis *Star Tribune*, 20 October 1998, p. 1A.

157. Bill Hillsman interview, 26 August 1999.

158. Conrad deFiebre, Bob von Sternberg, and Dane Smith, "Shift in Poll Creates Some Political Ripple," Minneapolis *Star Tribune*, 21 October 1998, p. 1B.

159. Coleman for Governor Campaign, "Only One," 1998. Videocassette of paid commercial obtained from KTCA-TV, Minneapolis. Available on the Internet at http://www.ktca.org/election98/adwatch.html.
160. Conrad deFiebre, Bob von Sternberg, and Dane Smith, "Shift in Poll Creates Some Political Ripple."
161. Randy Skoglund, Republican Party official and Coleman campaign worker, 18 August 1999, telephone interview by the author, Mahtomedi, MN, to Minneapolis, MN.
162. Patrick Sweeney, "Ventura: Consider Legalizing Prostitution," *St. Paul Pioneer Press,* 22 October 1998, p. 1A.
163. Patrick Sweeney, "Ventura Wrestles with Prostitution Question," *St. Paul Pioneer Press,* 23 October 1998, p. 1B.
164. Sweeney, "Ventura: Consider Legalizing Prostitution," p. 1A.
165. Ibid.
166. Nick Coleman, "Ventura's Straight Talk Merits Respect," *St. Paul Pioneer Press,* 26 October 1998, p. 1C.
167. Patricia Lopez-Baden, "Candidates Trade Volleys in Dispute on Gay Marriage," Minneapolis *Star Tribune,* 24 October 1998, p. 1B.
168. Chris Georgacas interview, 4 August 1999.
169. Dane Smith, "Candidates Do Very Little Debating," Minneapolis *Star Tribune,* 25 October 1998, p. 1B.
170. Bill Hillsman, "Reform Party Ad," 1998. Videocassette loaned to the author by North Woods Advertising, Minneapolis, from 2 October 1999 until 11 November 1999.
171. Corey Kiefer, "Citizen Jesse."
172. Bill Hillsman interview, 26 August 1999.
173. "Star Tribune Endorsements" (editorial), Minneapolis *Star Tribune,* 25 October 1998, p. 24A.
174. Ibid.
175. Dane Smith, "Norm Coleman," Minneapolis *Star Tribune,* 25 October 1998, p. 14A; Robert Whereatt, "Hubert Humphrey III," Minneapolis *Star Tribune,* 25 October 1998, p. 15A.
176. Jim Ragsdale, "Campaign 1998 Minnesota," *St. Paul Pioneer Press,* 27 October 1998, p. 2C.
177. Jim Ragsdale, "Interest Groups Roll Out Last-Minute Election Ads," *St. Paul Pioneer Press,* 28 October 1998, p. 4C.
178. "Ad Name: 'Believe,'" *St. Paul Pioneer Press,* 21 October 1998, p. 3B.
179. League of Women Voters, "Blake Debate." Video recording of the 27 October 1998 debate sponsored by the League of Women Voters. Loaned to the author from the League of Women Voters from 14 January until 13 March 2000.
180. Ibid.
181. Ibid.
182. Ibid.
183. Ibid.
184. Bill Hillsman, "Jesse Action Figure," 1998. Videocassette loaned to the author by North Woods Advertising, Minneapolis, from 2 October 1999 until 11 November 1999.

185. Bill Hillsman interview, 26 August 1999.

186. Joe Soucheray, "The, uh, Mind Keeps Up His Fearless Charge," *St. Paul Pioneer Press*, 28 October 1998, p. 1C.

187. Ibid.

188. "The Jesse Ventura Effect," *St. Paul Pioneer Press*, 29 October 1998, p. 14A.

189. Jack B. Coffman, "Candidates Cordial as Campaigns Crisscross," *St. Paul Pioneer Press*, 29 October 1998, p. 1A.

190. Patrick Sweeney and Jim Ragsdale, "Governor Candidates Fan Out to Light Fire Under Faithful," Minneapolis *Star Tribune*, 30 October 1998, p. 1A.

191. Bill Hillsman interview, 26 August 1999.

192. Ibid.

193. Bill Hillsman, "Drive to Victory," 1998. Videocassette loaned to the author by North Woods Advertising, Minneapolis, from 2 October 1999 until 11 November 1999.

194. Bob von Sternberg interview, 18 July 1999.

195. Tony Carlson, DFL activist and Ventura campaign volunteer, 20 July 1999, telephone interview by the author, Cambridge, MA, to Minneapolis, MN.

196. Dean Barkley interview, 3 August 1999.

197. KSTP-TV, St. Paul, "Last Minute Campaigning." Aired 31 October 1998. Videocassette of newscast given to author by KSTP-TV.

198. Ibid.

199. Ibid.

200. Jesse Ventura, *I Ain't Got Time to Bleed*, pp. 167–168.

201. Jim Ragsdale and Patrick Sweeney, "Campaign Reaches Peak," *St. Paul Pioneer Press*, 1 November 1998, p. 1A.

202. Bill Hillsman, "Thinker," 1998. Videocassette loaned to the author by North Woods Advertising, Minneapolis, from 2 October 1999 until 11 November 1999.

203. Bill Hillsman interview, 26 August 1999.

204. Dane Smith and Robert Whereatt, "Ventura Wins," Minneapolis *Star Tribune*, 4 November 1998, p. 1A.

205. Ibid.

3

ANALYZING VENTURA'S VICTORY

To begin to comprehend Ventura's triumph, it is instructive to distinguish between two distinct questions. The first: Who voted for Ventura and why? Simply put, what was the source of his support in the election? The second question is, how did Ventura's campaign overcome the obstacles that traditionally constrain third parties? Answering these two questions in detail, piece by piece, using many different sources to dissect the race, will set the groundwork for the following chapter's discussion of the election's implications for political science theory.

Explaining Who Voted for Ventura and Why:
Eight Theories

Who would vote for a former "sports entertainer," who achieved fame as a professional wrestling villain, who possessed minimal education or government experience? Apparently, 37 percent of the voters of Minnesota would and did. The question is *why*. Who were these voters? And why did Ventura appeal to them?

It seems as though everyone—media pundits, political commentators, Reform Party members, Republicans and Democrats alike, even political scientists—has an explanation for Jesse Ventura's victory. Some of these have become so common as to be accepted as fact in the popular culture and, worse, in the media. A few—eight, in my opinion—are worthy of analysis. These can be parsed into distinct hypotheses and then analyzed scientifically. We now examine each in turn.

The New Voters Theory

Minnesota is one of seven states with a same-day voter registration law.[1] Most people knew that Ventura won because he was able to get a great number of people to register to vote on election day—that was, in fact, part of the Reform Party's strategy. However, hitherto nobody knew how many of the 332,540 people (15.7 percent of the total vote) who registered on election day actually cast their ballot for Ventura. The Voter News Service exit pollsters did not ask interviewees if they had registered that day, and of course the polling stations themselves did not ask anyone registering that day for whom they were planning to vote. The only data available from the Secretary of State's office was the Ventura vote by precinct (with over 1,000 precincts in the state) and the number of same-day registrants by precinct.[2] Using a complicated mathematical procedure known as ecological inference, it is possible to derive from this data an accurate estimation of the same-day registrant vote that went for Ventura.[3] This derived estimate is 69.6 percent. That is, Ventura won approximately 225,184 of the 332,540 same-day registrant votes, or 10.9 percent of the total turnout. Considering that Ventura won the election by just over 60,000 votes, there is no doubt that the presence of a same-day registration option was crucial to his victory. Were it not for Minnesota's abnormal electoral rules permitting voting registration on election day, then, Minnesota would be under the administration of Norm Coleman, and Ventura would be an also-ran in Minnesota and unknown to the nation.

The Youth Vote Theory

One explanation of Ventura's success that is popular among members of the Reform Party is that of a profound youth vote: that the young people of Minnesota—college students and those high school students old enough to vote, a generation eminently sober to life's realities and unimpressed by empty rhetoric or patronizing nonsense—saw in Jesse a straight-talking guy, in simpatico with their lives, concerns, and worldview in ways no "professional politician" could ever be. They were impressed by his refusal to dance around the truth, and they came out in droves to put him in office. This was exactly what Rick McCluhan, chair of the Reform Party in Minnesota, said during an interview:

> This generation has been told during its maturation that they'll do less well than their parents. They've been condemned as inadequate. Many

of them have fallen behind the technocrats. They're the inheritors of a $4 trillion debt and a damaged environment. They're too cynical to buy manufactured people now. This generation gave Minnesota this election.[4]

The example almost always cited is Ventura's promise at the University of Minnesota to do away with government tuition assistance, which was met with wild cheers from the students. Bill Cooper lamented this reaction: "I saw him go down to the University of Minnesota and promise to eliminate student aid, and they cheered. . . . There's so much media attention on personal problems, how horrible politics are. It's denigrated the political process. A significant number of young people think political contributions go to the candidate and you [the candidate] get to keep the money."[5] Mike Landy, an activist in the Reform Party in St. Cloud, saw the youth mobilization more positively: "My son was excited about politics for the first time, to elect somebody who wasn't a politician."[6]

Gene Franchett, a Reform Party member in the Twin Cities, told an anecdote that illustrated this apparent enthusiasm among young people:

I put up signs for Jesse. A week later, they're all gone. I called the police. I thought the other parties had taken them. The police told me that the young people are taking them because they want them as souvenirs. That's when I thought that something different was going on.[7]

This version of events—young people "rocking the vote"—is popular and somewhat widespread, quite possibly due to the tendency of teenagers and college students to tell anyone who would listen that they, too, came out to vote to do their part in making Jesse their next governor.[8] This theory has become so widely accepted that the DFL leadership began a new outreach program for young people after the election, hoping to capture these voters in future elections. "The message is, look, we screwed up and we know it, but we're going to do better next time," Kathy Czar said about the apparent newfound political interest in young people.[9]

But as with many things, the myth has more impressive proportions than reality. It is correct that without the amount of the youth vote that he won, Ventura could not have won the election. But, on the other hand, if the entire youngest voting bracket had stayed home on election day, then, according to the exit polls, Coleman would have won by a tenth of a point (and this assumes both that the exit polling is not off by at least a tenth of a percent—which it probably is—and also that the preponderance of the makeup of the youngest voting bracket in the exit poll—18 to 29—is not people well into their twenties and thus not really "youth"; that is, the size of the actual "youth" group—people from 18 to about 23 or so—could actually be quite small). Consider Table 3.1.

Table 3.1   Vote Breakdown by Age

Age	Percentage of Total Vote	Percentage of Age Group Vote Going to Ventura/ Percentage of Total Vote that Was Both from the Age Group and for Ventura	Percentage of Age Group Vote Going to Humphrey/ Percentage of Total Vote that Was Both from the Age Group and for Humphrey	Percentage of Age Group Vote Going to Coleman/ Percentage of Total Vote that Was Both from the Age Group and for Coleman
18–29	15.7	48.5/7.6	18/2.8	31.4/4.9
30–44	35	42.9/15	22.2/7.8	34.4/12
45–59	29.3	31.8/9.3	32.3/9.5	35/10.1
60 or over	20	23.3/4.7	40.7/8.1	36.1/7.2

Source: 1998 Voter News Service exit poll.

As Table 3.1 indicates, Ventura did indeed carry young voters. Among 18–29 year olds, Ventura garnered 48.5 percent of the vote, more than any other candidate and the greatest share of any age group by any candidate. But Ventura was also the most popular candidate among 30–44 year olds, getting 42.9 percent of their votes, and a greater share of his total 37 percent of the vote came from that group (about 15 percent) and the 45–59 age group (about 9.3 percent) than from the youth (about 7.6 percent). So, although Ventura definitely was popular among young voters, it was not the sort of "revolution" that many people have believed happened—there was plenty of support for Jesse Ventura in other age groups as well.

The Theory of Dudes

Another explanation of Ventura's win falls under the umbrella of what will be referred to as the Theory of Dudes.[10] Interviewees who articulated this explanation hypothesized that Ventura won disproportionate support from a group they often referred to as "dudes"—a whole group of people, mostly white men, who have traditionally made their living working with their hands, who probably do not have much education beyond high school, and whose jobs (and without getting into pop psychology and other pretensions, their identities) have been disappearing at a precipitous rate, as jobs go overseas while their specialized skills remain, not easily redirected at another line of work.

According to this theory, these people saw in Ventura a man who was not overly fancy, who had made his living with his hands, had served in the military, was a union member (in the actors guild), and who knew how to relate to them on their level. These are guys who smoke and drink beer, who hunt and fish, who change their own oil and sometimes build their own race cars. The *Pioneer Press* seemed to suggest this when it printed an article proclaiming Humphrey and Coleman to be wary of "Everyman Ventura." The "dudes theory" proposes that these likeminded individuals came out to vote for someone they saw as one of their own, something they had not been able to do with previous candidates, and it was they who put Ventura into office.

Kathy Czar remembers a moment of clarity in the campaign when she and a friend were listening to Ventura discussing the perennial Minnesota political subject of Native American spear-fishing rights: "When Jesse was campaigning, he was talking about how the Indian tribes should have to fish in their traditional manners all the way, in birch bark canoes and so forth. Then he talked about how his traditional style of fishing was with explosives dropped in the water. A friend of mine said, 'That's bar talk.' And that's his secret: He talks like he's in a bar."[11] Bill Hillsman's strategy of targeting this sort of people—blue-collar workers who maybe have a lake cabin, a boat, a motorcycle, or a snowmobile—was partially born of a parallel sentiment; when interviewed for this book he said, "This was the first time these guys felt like they had a horse in the race."

According to these interviewees, "dudes" are lower-education, lower-income white men. For analysis purposes, "dudes" are defined as white men with high-school education or less and with family incomes of $50,000 or less (the exit poll questionnaire did not ask occupation).[12] Additionally, I contrasted the vote choice of this group with their low-income, low-education female counterparts and with the vote choice of what I define as male and female "nondudes"—those with at least a four-year college degree and earning $75,000 or more.[13]

The results of this analysis, shown in Table 3.2, lend credence to this theory. Though it's not known if this group voted for Ventura out of frustration or because of some love of Ventura's perceived working-class connection—it's impossible to know for sure either way—it is abundantly clear that Ventura had a greater appeal among the working class, and more allure among men than among women.

Table 3.2   Vote of "Dudes" and "Nondudes"

	Percentage of Group Voting for Ventura
Male "Dudes" (high school or less, income less than $50k)	48.2
Female "Dudes" (high school or less, income less than $50k)	42.4
Male "Nondudes" (college or more, income $75k or more)	30.3
Female "Nondudes" (college or more, income $75k or more)	21.4

Source: 1998 Voter News Service exit poll.
Note: The interviews seemed to suggest that this sort of person was white. In addition, Minnesota is overwhelmingly white (94 percent), and so to make the sample as unified as possible and avoid any distortions from the few minorities surveyed, only the white respondents' data was used for this section.

Table 3.2 shows that this view of Ventura's success—both Ventura's appeal to male voters and his appeal to lower socioeconomic groups—is supported by the evidence. He won 48.2 percent of the dudes' votes, compared to the 30.3 percent he won among male nondudes. It seems, though, that the socioeconomic understanding of his electoral support should be extended to female dudes as well. Ventura enjoyed greater support among men in both the lower and the upper education and income categories, which would make it seem that he appealed to not just the lower education and income men but to men of all sorts, more so than women. It's true that he got his greatest support in the male dude demographic, but "female dudes," so to speak, while not voting for him to the same degree as did males, were still 10 to 20 percent more likely to vote for Ventura than their nondude counterparts, and, moreover, they gave Ventura more than his average (37 percent) support, whereas male and female nondudes did not.[14]

It can be said, then, that there is a fair amount of truth to the Theory of Dudes. Although we don't know *why* they voted for Ventura over the other two candidates, it is true that people with lesser levels of education and income flocked to him. And, perhaps not surprising given his testosterone-juiced manner (or perhaps because of his libertarian stance, something known to attract men and repulse women), Ventura's support was markedly stronger among men than women among both groups. But even more marked was the difference in his support from both male and female dudes than from male and female nondudes, which suggests that Ventura did in fact have a great appeal to working-class people, regardless of gender.

As with the aforementioned Youth Vote Theory, though, the Theory of Dudes is correct with certain caveats. First, while Ventura certainly was most popular among lower-education, lower-income white males, he was also very popular among their female counterparts, which suggests that his appeal was not as much related to gender as to socioeconomic group. That said, he was also much more popular among male nondudes than female nondudes, which suggests that his gender appeal cut across class lines.

The Disaffected Democrat Theory

Another hypothesis of why Ventura won is that some DFLers were offended by Skip Humphrey's refusal to honor the party's endorsement of Mike Freeman and so threw their votes to Ventura. Alan Shilepsky, the Reform Party candidate for secretary of state, said that during his own failed campaign, he found such people: "I ran into a guy on a drive around, he's a Democrat. He was so mad about Skip taking the endorsement [process victory away from Freeman] that he was willing to back Ventura."[15]

A good example of such a person is Tony Carlson, a lifelong DFL Party activist and an unabashed liberal. He supported Mike Freeman, and when Skip Humphrey won the primary and took the nomination, he was as mad as a hornet. "After the primary, I didn't feel that the candidate represented our party," he says. He took his consternation and joined the Ventura campaign. His move might sound odd to others, but he found no trouble justifying it to his liberal self. He says of Ventura:

> He's a champion of working people. He's a union guy. He's pro-choice. He supports public education. He supports affirmative action in some cases. He's been on the wrong side of the law. He got dirty to earn his living. Neither of the other candidates had ever been in a union, and neither was a veteran. Ventura was both. He sure sounds like a Democrat to me.[16]

The Humphrey campaign made a big stink about insisting that Ventura be invited to the debates, because they thought that Ventura would be a spoiler for Coleman. Of course, he would have been invited anyway, and it was for the most part Humphrey who was hurt by his presence there.

While it is impossible to tell how many DFLers abandoned Humphrey out of anger (and not, say, because they felt that Ventura simply better represented the working class, or because they liked his grassroots populism), we do know that Ventura ultimately captured a greater share of the DFL base than he did of the Republican base: He won 31.7 percent of the DFL vote and 28.5 percent of the Republican vote (in a Democratic state). Thus, the conventional wisdom that a fiscally conservative Reform Party candidate would hurt a Republican more than a Democrat failed in this case. Table 3.3 shows the breakdown of voting for the candidates based on registered party affiliation.

Table 3.3   Vote by Party Identification

	Ventura	Humphrey	Coleman
Independent	52	17.3	28.3
Democrat	31.7	56.6	11.1
Republican	28.5	4.7	66.7

Source: 1998 Voter News Service exit poll.

Note: A small percentage of voters cast their ballots for someone other than one of the three main candidates; hence the sum of the votes per party affiliation is in each case slightly less than one hundred.

The explanation for the greater levels of DFL defection might revolve around Skip Humphrey's performance as an unexciting campaigner who failed to rouse the troops. Related to this might be an extension of the Theory of Dudes, which is to say Jesse Ventura captured the imaginations of some traditional Democratic voters—blue-collar, lower-income people—because he seemed so much like one of their own.

Ventura's ability to pull Democrats probably intersected with his appeal to lower socioeconomic groups (discussed earlier), and in some regard it also made the election seem that of a true populist. Ventura, in truth a wealthy man, was able to portray himself as some kind of working-class hero, and he even turned his lack of government experience (other than a stint in a weak suburban mayorship) into a populist advantage by pointing to his more than twenty years in the private sector (versus what he depicted as his "professional politician" opponents' having spent the vast majority of their time feeding at the public trough of working people's taxes).

Regardless of what caused the great defection of Democrats, we can see that Ventura "stole" more from Humphrey's base than Coleman's.

Coleman, originally thought to be doomed by Ventura's rise, held his core much better than Humphrey.

The Suburbanite Theory

If the election results are drawn by precinct on a state map, Ventura's area of victory is a donut shape around the Twin Cities, in line with the suburbs that Ed Gross had targeted earlier for the campaign. Coleman did best in the "Republican L," and Humphrey did well in the Iron Range and the Twin Cities. (Table 3.4 shows votes for Ventura by Region. See also Appendix A for a map of the vote by county, which does not capture the voting pattern nearly as accurately as would a map of the vote by precinct.)

Table 3.4 Votes for Ventura by Region

	White Men	White Women
Twin Cities	41.4	32.1
Metro (suburbs)	46.3	44.9
Democratic Areas (Iron Range)	36.2	25.9
Republican Areas (Republican "L")	30.5	37.3

Source: 1998 Voter News Service exit poll.

The Suburbanite Theory suggests that Ventura received heavy support in the suburbs of Minneapolis and St. Paul not simply because he spent most of his time and campaign money there but because the voters there could afford to take chances. Residents of these areas were for the most part the greatest beneficiaries of the booming economy and stock market, and in that regard they were able to take a chance on someone like Ventura. Jack Meeks, one of Coleman's inner circle of advisers, was asked if he thought there was some sort of economic or social tension propelling Ventura. "No," he said, "quite the opposite. I think when times are this good you can afford to take your voting lightly."[17] Farmers and Iron Rangers, in contrast, had real problems and worries and could not take a chance on someone with no real government experience. It is interesting to note that while Ventura drew heavily from the state's Democratic base, he fared much worse among Iron Range Democrats, whose constant economic concerns could perhaps not allow them to vote in favor of a candidate simply because he was going to stir the pot.

Because there is a second conceivable reason for Ventura's success in the suburbs—that Ventura's ads specifically targeted them—it is impossible to know which bears more of the explanation, and it makes for a chicken-and-egg problem. Were these suburbanites Ventura voters because they could afford to tweak the political system, or did they vote for Ventura because he took his Drive to Victory through their towns? Similarly, did the outlying Republican and Democrat areas not vote for him because they were skeptical of him, or was it because the Ventura campaign did not spend any advertising on those areas?

The Anger Theory

We now come to a sixth theory, one that posits that Ventura was a channel for people's anger. His candidacy was a way for angry people to strike out at the system. As Arne Carlson put it when interviewed for this book, "He got what people call a protest vote, but it's ill-defined. Nobody knows what they're angry about. There's just a lot of angry people out there."

One way to tell people's dissatisfaction with the status quo (but by no means a complete way) is through their assessment of their personal financial situation. Those who see themselves as worse off since the previous election should, according to this theory, vote for Ventura. As can be seen in Table 3.5, they do.

Table 3.5 Personal Financial Situation of Voters Since the Previous Election

	Percentage of Electorate	Ventura	Humphrey	Coleman
Better	42.2	39.3	28.9	31.3
Worse	13.2	46.4	21.6	30.9
Same	44.6	32.2	28.9	37.7

Source: 1998 Voter News Service exit poll.

Note: A small percentage of voters cast their ballots for someone other than one of the three main candidates; hence the sum of the votes per candidate is in each case slightly less than one hundred.

Ventura won this group hands-down, with over 46 percent of their vote. But he also handily beat the other two candidates among people who saw themselves as better off than before, of whom there were far more in such cozy economic times. The only group he did not win were those who saw their personal financial situation as the same as before. It is not wrong, then, to say that Ventura probably won the bulk of protest votes, but that was hardly his only source of support. However, because Coleman won among those who saw their situation as the same, and because there were slightly more of them (44.6 percent versus 42.2 percent who saw their situation as better), if Ventura had not managed such a decisive victory among the smaller group (13.2 percent) who saw their situation as worse, the election result might have been different.[18]

Candidate-Based Vote Theory

Another hypothesis that jibes with all the other explanations advanced heretofore holds that Ventura won based on his personal appeal—especially compared to the other two candidates. If Skip Humphrey ended up being seen as out of touch and Norm Coleman came across as a slick politician, or vice versa, Jesse Ventura may have seemed to many voters an arbiter of common sense and honesty. A 1999 poll found that one-third of Americans ranked honesty as the far-and-away most important quality they look for in someone running for office.[19] Maybe it's not really a stretch to accept that Jesse Ventura was the best candidate in this regard. Indeed, Governor Carlson felt that the one thing Ventura succeeded in doing during the campaign was painting his opponents as bad people. He was nearly furious about it:

> The fundamental problem with the debates was that Ventura would challenge the integrity and honesty of both Coleman and Humphrey as well as virtually every political figure in American history, and neither Coleman nor Humphrey would respond. Their pollsters and advisers had told them to ignore Ventura and not offend his base of voters. People watching the debates were dumbfounded. How could anyone sit there and have their integrity challenged and remain silent? It made no sense. It allowed Ventura to define both of them as dishonest career politicians, and that was a total untruth. But what was true is that they came across as over-managed, too cautious, and somewhat unreal.[20]

Ventura may have been seen as having the best personal qualities, then, because he made a point of contrasting the other candidates with his straight talk and commonsensical plan for governing. Reform Party Chairperson Rick McCluhan described exactly this when he said, "Jesse made government an issue by pointing to these stupid things going on in the campaign and saying, 'See what I mean? See what I mean? See what I mean?'"[21] Former DFL chair Dick Senese, a professor of political science at St. Olaf College, remarked, "Minnesotans have always responded well to strong individuals who speak their minds." Alan Shilepsky, who ran for secretary of state in the Reform Party, recalled, "There was this 'anti-the-other-two' thing. 'Retaliate in '98' is a real telling slogan. There is this popular resentment of political elites."[22]

Moreover, in addition to coming across as an honest, regular guy, Ventura is an incredibly charismatic person. Mavis Huddle, his campaign secretary, says, "He has a charisma about him that just captures an entire audience."[23] He has a tremendous stage presence, an enormous shape, and a distinctive voice. One DFLer who studied acting in college was blown away by Ventura's excellent control of his body language and speaking.[24]

In a St. Cloud State University survey taken before the election, respondents were given reasons for voting for the three candidates (where multiple responses were allowed and the value is the percent of respondents responding that the variable given was a reason to vote for the candidate); 44 percent of respondents said that Ventura's character was a reason to vote for him, whereas only 27 percent said that of Coleman, and 28 percent of Humphrey.[25]

These things put together probably created a positive situation for Ventura. Bob von Sternberg, the respected *Star Tribune* reporter who covered Ventura, used deliberate exaggeration to explain what he felt was the general public sentiment: "Why did people vote for him? Skip seemed like a dope. And Norm Coleman is a party-switching snake. You got this third guy who's not a Neanderthal, who is smart. I think a lot of people said, 'Oh, what the hell.'"[26]

Issue-Based Vote

How did Jesse Ventura do on the issues as compared to the other candidates? The exit pollers asked people to identify the single most important issue for them; the results of how they voted are shown in Table 3.6.

With the exception of abortion, Ventura did well compared to the other candidates in every issue category. On the issue of taxes, Ventura came remarkably close to beating Coleman—and so seems to have come across as a tax-cutter. He got 40 percent of the vote from the 29 percent of the electorate who said it was the most important issue for them (making it the most popular choice, followed by education at 25 percent), only slightly behind the 46.3 percent Coleman won from this group. Additionally, he was able to grab nearly 27 percent of those who thought education was the most important, almost half of the 57 percent

Table 3.6　Vote by Issue

Issue Most Important	Ventura	Humphrey	Coleman
Farm Policy	36.7	35	26.7
Gun Control	48.6	29.2	19.4
Abortion	13.1	16.3	70.6
Crime	56.8	21	22.2
Economy	45	25.5	28.2
Education	26.9	55.4	16
Taxes	40.3	12.3	46.3

Source: 1998 Voter News Service exit poll.
Note: A small percentage of voters cast their ballots for someone other than one of the three main candidates; hence the sum of the votes per issue is in each case slightly less than one hundred.

Skip Humphrey won in this category, and far ahead of the 14.8 percent Coleman won. Interestingly enough, he won over half of those who said crime was the most important issue, twice as much as either of his opponents. Even more fascinating is that he won the farm policy voters with 36.7 percent, which is surprising since Coleman did well in agricultural areas.[27] For people who said that gun control was most important to them, he beat both candidates, with 46 percent compared to the 25.4 percent the other two each won (it is reasonable to assume that there were differing interpretations on what exactly "gun control" meant—more of it, or less). Again, Ventura seems to have co-opted the issue from Coleman. And among those who said that the economy (jobs) was the most important issue, Ventura walked away with 43 percent of the 13 percent who said this. Moreover, on the issue of concealed weapons, Ventura again seemed to have co-opted the issue from Coleman, meaning that all the attacks and accusations of flip-flopping the Republican put up with over this issue was almost for nothing—Ventura got 52 percent of the vote from those who thought it should be easier to carry a concealed weapon, compared to Coleman's 35 percent. And it appears to have not hurt him on the flip side, as all three candidates got 33 percent of those who said that it should not be easier to carry a concealed weapon. Among those who opposed using public money to build a new sports stadium (which 83 percent of voters did), Ventura again won, garnering nearly 38 percent of the vote in this group (Coleman won among the 17 percent that did favor using public funds, with 39 percent of their vote).[28]

It is impossible to say that people voted for Ventura *because* of any of these issues—they may have thought, for example, that taxes were the most important issue and that Coleman had a better plan but voted for Ventura for a personal reason, such as his perceived honesty. It *is* fair to say that essentially none of Ventura's positions, to the extent that he had them, hurt him dramatically, and that he was able to appear credible enough on certain important issues that people were willing to vote for him, even if that issue was not their reason for choosing him.

In Sum

Ventura's support was wide and varied, but he drew especially on certain groups—the young, lower socioeconomic groups, and Democrats. The popular belief about his support among young people was overblown, as a greater share of his support actually came from older voters (though he did, in fact, win the young persons' vote). The biggest source of his victory came from suburban, lower-socioeconomic males and, to a lesser extent, females of the same type. It can reasonably be said, though, that because the election was so close, Ventura could not have won without at least some support from every distinct group.

Ventura also did well in attracting votes of people for whom different issues were important. That said, just because Ventura won the vote of someone for whom, say, taxes were the most important issue does not per se mean that that is why they voted for him; it simply means that when asked about which *issue* was most important, they had to name an *issue*—they were not saying why they voted the way they did. As was discussed, polling suggests that Ventura's personal qualities, far more than his public policy prescriptions, powered his campaign. Like many third-party candidates, the specifics of his platform were hazy. Ventura's relative paucity of specifics about any one issue (his plan for education: smaller class sizes) may have been redeemed by the economically plush circumstances in which the election took place.

The best amalgamation of reasons for this election's outcome might be to say that Ventura was able to become all things to all people. He was a protest candidate for those who desired one (at a time of presidential impeachment, for instance), yet he was also a winner, beating his opponents in head-to-head match-ups on a majority of the issues; in other words, he was simultaneously a legitimate candidate for regular, middle-of-the-road voters and a protest for voters at the margins. He was able to co-opt issues while not being hurt by them, partly because it is so hard to pigeonhole him on the political spectrum (he even took a plurality of the self-identified liberal vote).[29] He drew heavily on the young, but he also did well in every age group except those over sixty. Despite his fiscal conservatism—proposing that the state abandon its subsidies for child care—and how well he did among people who saw taxes as a priority, he captured a great number of Democrats.

Ventura's Success as a Third-Party Candidate

Absence of Economic and Social Tension

The central work on third parties in American politics is *Third Parties in America,* by Steven Rosenstone, Roy Behr, and Edward Lazarus. In it they link the appearance and rise of a third party with economic or social problems that are seen as being handled ineffectively by the two major parties.[30]

Minnesota was, if anything, the opposite of a troubled state. From 1990 to 1997, Minnesota per capita personal income rose nearly 36 percent.[31] Even in the context of the national economic expansion, Minnesota has done especially well: In 1997 it ranked thirteenth among the states in personal income per capita, up from seventeenth in 1990.[32]

Minnesota's unemployment has been below the national average for over a decade, and below 4 percent since 1994. In 1998, unemployment in the state barely averaged 2 percent, less than half the national average of 4.5 percent.[33] In May 1999, Minnesota tied with Nebraska as having the lowest unemployment in U.S. history.[34] And, as was said earlier, the state government was experiencing a budget surplus.

As for social tension, things were equally pleasant. The state's homicide rate, always near the bottom among the states, fell 32 percent from 1995 to 1997.[35] Only ten states had lower homicide rates; all of them, including Minnesota, were at 2.5 per 100,000 people or less.[36] The number of youth offenders had been falling since 1994.[37] Crimes that people might notice more readily—"quality-of-life crimes"—and might help engender a rebellion at the voting booth were down as well. Reported burglaries were down since 1993. So were reports of vandalism.[38] Moreover, in the election itself, crime was not particularly important; one survey by St. Cloud State University found that only 2 percent of voters rated a candidate's position on crime as an important reason to vote for or against him or her.[39]

The state has the highest rate of high school graduation in the nation.[40] Even volunteerism among high school students was up.[41] And so were test scores.[42] The 1996 *Children's Services Report Card* reported that under Governor Carlson's administration the state had successfully reduced the number of children in the state who were neglected, abused, exposed to alcoholism in their families, sexually active, or receiving AFDC.[43] Even the issue of public financing for a new sports stadium was probably far less important than people thought; despite the owners' continual demands for a new stadium, the legislature never gave serious consideration to proposals to do so, as the public had made its opposition clear.[44]

Given this absence of social or economic tension, in a time of unprecedented societal health where nothing would logically give way to a third-party movement, one must look elsewhere for the sources of Ventura's victory. They in large part lie in Minnesota's unique institutions.

Reduction of Third-Party Barriers

Third Parties in America reads like a veritable laundry list of the American electoral system's obstacles to third parties. But as with most things, Minnesota is an exception, as the state has rules and institutions that reduce, if not eliminate, most of these barriers. What's more, the playing field of Minnesota state politics is not radically different from that in other states—the changes are slight, and for those interested in changing or reforming the American political system, they hold important lessons.

Ballot Restrictions. Getting on the ballot is usually "an arduous task for third party contenders, even well-financed ones."[45] Each state sets its own access laws, which means that someone running for president must "overcome fifty-one different sets of bureaucratic hurdles."[46] Getting on the ballot usually requires petitions that must be circulated within a specific short time period, which varies from state to state—for instance, between the first of August and the first of September in Indiana. Some states require just a small number of signatures, like Tennessee's twenty-five, while others are more difficult, like the 5 percent of registered voters required in Montana and Oklahoma. In California in 1980, a candidate needed 100,000 signatures.[47] South Carolinians must record both their precinct and voter registration numbers with their signature, and New Hampshire requires signatures to be certified.[48] In 1984 the New Alliance Party ran Lenora Fulani on nearly every ballot in the country, but at a cost: The party estimates that 70 percent of the $2 million it collected went to finance the drive for petition signatures it needed.[49] And Eugene McCarthy, after his ballot drives and court battles, had only $100,000 left for media advertising in 1976.[50]

Not so in Minnesota, where any party that has won over 5 percent of the vote in the previous statewide election is considered a major party and is automatically on the ballot.[51] Thus, with Ross Perot's 24 percent in 1992 and Dean Barkley's Senate campaigns in 1994 and 1996 (winning 5 and 7 percent, respectively), Jesse Ventura was on the ballot as soon as he became the Reform Party nominee. In fact, Barkley ran for Senate the second time solely to secure major party status.[52] For a party running on a shoestring budget and with few volunteers to spare, having to gather signatures is a huge burden to have removed. What's more, in Minnesota the major party receiving the fewest number of votes in the previous election—here, the Reform Party—is first on the ballot in the next one, meaning that the first names voters read in 1998 when they picked up their ballots were Jesse Ventura and Mae Schunk.[53]

Financial Barriers. J. David Gillespie writes in *Politics at the Periphery* that "most third parties lack the resources to purchase access to the public via expensive newspaper, radio, and television advertising."[54] There are a variety of reasons for this. Many third parties tend to be composed of committed ideologues or reformers who do not have the personal resources or the networks to raise money.[55] Membership is often small, reducing its resource base. Moreover, because voting for a third party is a "wasted vote" in many people's minds, it is hard to get them to contribute to a losing cause. Similarly, the powerful interest groups with money to give—for example, business and labor—are tied to the major parties already and naturally prefer a party in power to one with little chance of winning, and one with unconventional policy prescriptions at that. Rosenstone, Behr, and Lazarus find in *Third Parties* that minor parties on average are able to afford one-twentieth the television and radio time of the major party nominees.[56] Stillborn third-party fundraising results in their ability to put out "only a fraction of the political advertising bought by the Democrats and the Republicans."[57]

For most third parties, then, money—a lack of it—kills their efforts before they even start. But, again, not so Minnesota. Minnesota's public financing system was created in 1974 as a post-Watergate innovation aimed at insulating Minnesota's politics from the perceived influence of private money.[58] Candidates who agree to participate in the public financing system are bound to raise no more than 20 percent of their spending limit from political action committees (PACs) and lobbyists.[59] As of mid-1998, Minnesota led the nation in the percentages of campaign expenditures paid for by public funds.[60] Daniel Elazar, the famous political culture guru; Wy Spano, a Minnesota political observer; and University of Minnesota professor of political science Virginia Gray write, "Minnesota has fashioned a system for choosing its political leaders which is less influenced by private economic interests than in any other state."[61] Since the advent of the system, public funds have actually grown as a percentage of the total expenditures in state elections.[62]

Before discussing Minnesota's own public financing system in greater detail, it is useful to consider federal election law, designed likewise after Watergate to reduce the influence of money on campaigns and voting. Many critics have come to see the Federal Election Campaign Act's allocation of massive sums of money to the two major parties as a system that further marginalizes challenges from third parties.[63] Rosenstone, Behr, and Lazarus call it "a major party protection act."[64] Because a party's fund allocation is on a prorated basis of the share of the vote it won from four years previous (if it tallied over 5 percent), its federal allocation is always far less than the money given to the two major parties.[65] Moreover, a minor party may receive funds *after* the election if it is on the ballot in at least ten states and receives 5 percent of the national vote; however, it is still bound to the pre-election fundraising limits of $1,000 from individuals. Additionally, since many effectively third-party challenges have been from "independents," people like Eugene McCarthy are left out. He had to petition the Federal Election Commission (FEC) to get an exception. The FEC took six weeks to decide, until mid-October 1976, and then ruled against him.[66] John Anderson did receive a favorable ruling in 1980, but, Rosenstone and his coauthors point out, his hope to borrow against his postelection federal subsidy was dashed by banks that feared their loans would be seen as illegal contributions if he defaulted.[67]

In contrast, Minnesota's public financing system works to the benefit of third parties. To qualify for the program, a party must have won at least 5 percent of the vote in the most recent statewide election and have raised at least $25,000. As discussed, Barkley ran for Senate again in 1996 to retain the Reform Party's major party status and eligibility for the program, and T-shirt sales at the state fair put the party over the fundraising minimum.

Through this system the Ventura campaign qualified for over $326,000 in public money, which allowed it to run four popular and effective television advertisements during the last week of the campaign. The system functions such that a party is responsible for getting a loan equal to the amount for which they qualify under the state's rules, and if in the election they get at least 5 percent of the vote, the loan is repaid by public money. In *I Ain't Got Time to Bleed,* Ventura, who sees conspiratorial undertones in most things that do not go his way, describes this pay-now, get-paid-back-later system as "a great example of how the good-old-boy network protects itself," since it does require a third party to find a loan on its own *before* the election. However, that one must secure a private loan before the state hands out money actually serves to keep flash-in-the-pan third parties, which may have garnered 5 percent in the previous election but will not make a repeat performance, from receiving public funds.[68]

In exchange for public money, the campaigns are constrained in their spending. This limit grows with each election to keep pace with increasing campaigning costs (and thus make the program attractive to candidates), and in the 1998 gubernatorial election it was $1.9 million (though it varied slightly by candidate, as explained below).

Virtually all candidates for office, from state representative to governor, agree to "play by the rules" of Minnesota's public financing system for their campaigns (U.S. Senate and House races are federal elections and thus are exempt from the program).[69]

Several reasons commonly are given for the popularity of the program. First, the spending limit is meant to be and is sufficient to run a competitive race, television ads and all, though there was some criticism during the 1998 race that the limit has not kept pace with the costs of campaigning.[70] The ability to run an effective campaign within the spending limits, to be able to run for governor on less than $2.5 million, is no doubt related to the fact that the state has only one major media market, which reaches fully 80 percent of the populace.[71] Moreover, the penalty for noncompliance is heavy. If a candidate raises and spends more than is allowed, he (or she) is no longer able to receive any public money at all. Moreover, his opponent is freed from the spending constraints but is still eligible for state payments.[72]

The money is paid out according to a complex system that blends proportionality and equality. There are two accounts in the public subsidy program. The first is the Party Account, which is funded by voluntary tax return check-off contributions of $5 by individual taxpayers. Taxpayers can select a party to which to contribute, and it does not cost them anything; the check-off simply redirects a portion of their existing taxes to this purpose. For state constitutional offices, the Party Account is funded from statewide taxes, but for individual legislative districts money put into the Party Account comes from that district alone, so it is entirely possible that one candidate in a highly partisan district might receive far more money than an opponent would. In the 1998 gubernatorial election, the DFL nominee received $293,262 from the Party Account, the Republican nominee $249,358, and the Reform Party nominee $16,539.[73] (This makes sense, as the Reform Party base is small whereas the DFL and GOP are competitive behemoths, though the Democratic base is generally considered to be larger.)

The second account is the General Account. Taxpayers can contribute to this instead of the Party Account as well (though they can choose to contribute to neither), and it receives $1,500,000 from the state budget each election year in addition to the check-off amount generated.[74] This money is split evenly among the candidates who both meet the requirements above and also garner over 5 percent of the vote in the general election; as mentioned, it is given out after the votes are counted. In the 1998 election, Humphrey, Coleman, and Ventura each received $310,282 from this account.[75]

If a candidate agrees to participate in the program (as 98 percent of registered candidates did in 1998), a spending limit is imposed.[76] For the gubernatorial election in 1998, the limit was $1,926,127;[77] however, Humphrey got a 20 percent increase because he had a contested primary, and Coleman and Ventura each were allowed a 10 percent increase because they were first-time candidates for statewide office.[78] Thus, the three candidates were limited to between $2.1 and $2.3 million. Both the Humphrey and the Coleman campaigns spent as close to the maximum as they could (both around $2.1 million); Ventura spent only slightly more than $626,000.[79]

It was late in the campaign when Steve Minn, later to become one of Ventura's advisers, located a bank willing to make the pre-election loan. Franklin National was confident that Ventura would top 5 percent (Ventura had just polled at 21 percent); just in case he did not, the Reform Party took out an insurance policy on the loan.[80]

From the two public financing accounts, Ventura received a total of $326,821, Coleman received $559,640, and Humphrey $603,544. Thus, the Reform Party was handicapped by the party check-off part of the program but aided by the egalitarian General Account. Ventura's campaign received 58 percent of the money Coleman's did and 54 percent of the money Humphrey's campaign was allocated. (Compare this to the less than 20 percent the Reform Party received in 2000 at the national level, a difficulty compounded by the cost of ballot access drives.)

As discussed, the Ventura campaign received its share of the public money late in the campaign. This turned out to be an advantage. Though Hillsman admits that he hadn't wanted to go without funding until so late in the campaign, he realizes now that "by not getting the money till the very end we had the advantage of being competitive with the other campaigns."[81] Their radio and TV commercials didn't air until the crucial final days of the campaign, when they did the most good.[82]

Further, whereas most third parties find it nearly impossible to raise money, the Ventura campaign was able to collect an additional $300,000 from citizens in innovative ways.[83] Approximately half of this amount was from T-shirt sales, an especially smart way to capitalize on Ventura's celebrity.[84] Donations amounting to $80,000 came from visitors to the campaign's website.[85] Because these were credit card payments (versus checks), they were immediately available for use in the late stages of the campaign. Thus, the Ventura campaign was able to raise and spend almost 30 percent of what the other two campaigns did. And since Ventura did not really have to defend himself against attacks from the other two or from the media, only a small amount of his precious financial resources went to "damage control." Additionally, by concentrating their campaign in the Twin Cities, where Hillsman, working off his targeting data, knew their potential voters were, the Ventura campaign was able to spend entirely within this single major media market, thus avoiding the costs of radio and TV ads in outlying areas as well as the expense (and time) of traveling to the far reaches of the state to charm constituencies, as Coleman did with the farming regions and Humphrey did with the Iron Range.[86]

It should be noted that the Ventura campaign lacked the benefit of "independent expenditures"—spending by interest groups or soft money spending by the parties. Ventura did not receive any such support. The Republican Party spent over $5 million on the Coleman campaign, the DFL Party over $3 million.[87] The Minnesota Reform Party was able to spend barely $14,000 on the campaign.[88] The national Reform Party, allowed to contribute $20,000, demurred.[89] No interest groups backed Ventura or ran ads for him, as the business groups did for Coleman and the teachers unions did for Humphrey. Ventura, however, turned this into as much of an advantage as he could by making a constant issue about his refusal to accept any money or endorsements from any PACs or interest groups.

Ventura's campaign had only one paid staffer, could not afford to run polls, and did not even have a fax machine.[90] But public financing allowed the campaign to overcome all these obstacles and capture people's attention in the late part of the campaign. The irony, of course, is that Jesse Ventura, a man who spent the greater part of his time on the campaign trail raging against government programs, rode into office with the help of a government program. He himself acknowledged as much when asked how important he thought the public financing system was to his victory, saying, "Well, if we hadn't gotten our money, we couldn't have put our TV ads on, and [that's what] really gave us the boost at the end."[91]

Debate Participation. Perhaps the greatest obstacle facing third-party candidates is their exclusion from official debates. An inability to appear in debates with the Republican and Democrat candidates exacerbates the legitimacy problems that third parties typically face. Ross Perot was able to use his own personal fortune to create enough of a stir that he was included in three of the fall 1992 presidential debates. However, most third-party candidates "cannot beg their way on the debate stage."[92] McCarthy was left out in 1976. Ronald Reagan did debate John Anderson in 1980, but Jimmy Carter refused to participate, which had the effect of delegitimizing Anderson's candidacy.[93] Most recently, Perot was excluded in 1996, and Ralph Nader and Pat Buchanan were excluded in 2000.

Again, Minnesota's unique institutions gave Ventura's campaign a break and helped him overcome yet another obstacle that traditionally blocks third parties. Because of the Reform Party's legal status in Minnesota as a major party, Ventura was included in the debates from the outset. The League of Women Voters of Minnesota, sponsor of three of the six televised debates, uses this "major party" criterion in extending debate invitations.[94] "It's only fair to invite someone if they represent a major party," said a spokeswoman for the League.[95] That a candidate represents a major party suggests that he or she has some standing in the state and has a chance of being elected, and thus the party deserves to be represented in the debates and the public deserves to see what the candidate has to say.[96] Indeed, it was the League of Women Voters who had decided to invite Anderson to participate in the debate that Carter boycotted.[97] Additionally, other debate sponsors in Minnesota followed the League's example, primarily through their contact in a group called the Minnesota Compact. Designed to "raise the level of political discourse," the Minnesota Compact is a nonprofit, nonpartisan organization of civic and media organizations. It includes the League of Women Voters, the Minnesota News Council, the Humphrey Institute of Public Affairs, and several local colleges.[98] It strives to bring truthfulness to political campaigns, to involve more citizens in politics, and to help structure the debates.[99] To this end, it also was the impetus behind the "Adwatch" features in both major newspapers that appeared regularly to discuss the candidates' political ads and to expose the level of veracity within them, a feature that could only have served to reinforce Ventura's image of truthful common sense above the muck of dishonest and shallow partisan politics. The League of Women Voters is the primary sponsor of the Compact, and because of this and the general belief that the League is a leader in conducting political debates, the other debate-sponsoring organizations follow the League's lead and use the same criteria, inviting all legally defined major parties.[100]

Yet again, Minnesota's open institutional electoral arrangements, both governmental and civic, came to Ventura's aid. His inclusion in the debates cannot be underestimated. As has been discussed, he performed extremely well, appearing above the fray (mostly because Humphrey and Coleman ignored him) with his commonsense approach to government. And as Kathy Czar, who studied acting in college, pointed out, his stage presence was tremendous. Indeed, it was during the debate season that his poll standing began to rise dramatically. (See the figure in Appendix B for specifics on this trend.)

Media Coverage. Rosenstone, Behr, and Lazarus find another important barrier to third parties—and maybe the most important when one thinks about it: media coverage, both its absence and its tone. They write, "The primary reason third party candidates receive so little coverage is that broadcasters and publishers do not think they warrant attention. Nearly two out of three newspaper editors thought that their readers had little interest in third party candidates in 1980."[101] James M. Perry of the *Wall Street Journal* put it this way:

> We base [our decision] on the simple proposition that readers don't want to waste their time on someone who won't have a role in the campaign. We're not going to run a page-one spread on a fringe candidate. We don't have a multiparty system. Until we do, nobody's going to cover these candidates.[102]

There is a certain circular logic to how the media (and hence the public's conscience) deals with multiparty politics, which amounts to "It won't happen, so let's not help it happen." Media coverage, or lack of it, becomes a self-fulfilling prophecy for a third party's performance. In Minnesota, however, because of the Reform Party's official status as a major party, the media, generally well regarded for its quality and public-interest orientation, felt obliged to give Ventura his share of coverage. Longtime *Star Tribune* reporter Bob von Sternberg explained how he got assigned the Ventura beat: "I'm not a political reporter. We divided up the gubernatorial candidates. We usually don't cover minor

parties, but since the Reform Party had major party status, we decided
to cover Jesse. The political specialists went onto Norm and Skip, and
I got thrown with Jesse."[103] The amount of coverage given to Ventura
was probably aided by his unique biography, not to mention his irasci-
bility. As Mike Freeman put it, "He was new, he was clever, he was
funny, he made good copy."[104]

Compared to most third-party candidates, Ventura received a great
deal of media coverage. The *Star Tribune* archives from July to November 3, 1998, contain 368 articles, editorials, or letters to the editor
mentioning Coleman, 473 mentioning Humphrey, and 228 mentioning
Ventura. The *St. Paul Pioneer Press* archives for this same period contain 460 articles, editorials, or letters to the editor mentioning Humphrey,
525 mentioning Coleman, and 238 mentioning Ventura. Thus, in terms
of pure quantity, Ventura was able to get about half the press coverage
of the other two over the course of the race (a dreamy scenario for most
third-party candidates) and a much greater percentage as his numbers
continued to rise throughout the race.[105]

Public and Press Antipathy. Rosenstone, Behr, and Lazarus write that the
press often does more than simply ignore candidates running from third
parties; they are often hostile to them.[106] The media's failure to turn
against Ventura runs against third-party theory, and the importance of it
should not be underestimated. This has something to do with Jesse himself. That Jesse Ventura succeeded where Perot failed is in part due to
what would seem to be a drag on his credibility: his prominence as a
professional wrestler. Inasmuch as they were both political amateurs
who had interesting biographies, the two men bear similarity. A key difference, though, and one that goes beyond the mere celebrity that Ventura brought with him, was the specific nature of his fame, which created a unique case for media treatment.

Third Parties in America describes Perot's rise and fall in the 1992
presidential race as typical of third-party candidates, quoting a *Time*
magazine article in June of that year:

> Perot enjoyed a honeymoon of sorts—an initial period during which
> reports on [his] candidacy were overwhelmingly favorable, even up-
> beat. Initial stories focused on the myth of Ross Perot and the public's
> enthusiasm for his candidacy: the thousands of phone calls that poured
> into headquarters each day and how "across the country people on
> their own are trying to get Perot on the ballot" (Jamie Gangel on
> NBC's *Today,* March 16, 1992). Perot graced the cover of all the
> weekly news magazines. *Time*'s May 25 cover, for example, read,

"President Perot?" The media widely reported on Perot's standing as frontrunner in the polls. . . . Then the coverage turned sour. Talk show hosts pushed for specifics. Journalists focused on Perot's shallow understanding of the issues, his inexperience, and his authoritarian style. . . . The electorates' opinion of Ross Perot grew increasingly negative.[107]

Third Parties in America shows this pattern as typical—initial adulation as "a breath of fresh air" turning to harsh scrutiny amidst "no chance to win," in the media and in turn in the public conscience. John Anderson experienced the same phenomena in 1980—a favorite of the press for a moment before being cast as a wasted vote.[108] Rosenstone and co-authors illustrates a similar pattern for every third-party presidential candidate except Strom Thurmond and Henry Wallace, in which the candidates experience an initial surge in popularity that falls precipitously as people become convinced that they are wasting their votes.[109]

Ventura's legitimacy and candidacy might have been undercut by some of the same factors that undercut Perot—a poor understanding of public policy and lack of experience (not to mention his temper)—if the media had shifted their gaze to him more pointedly. After all, Ventura announced his candidacy for governor almost a year before the election, leaving plenty of time for scrutiny. But because everything about Ventura was treated as a big joke in the established media, he never received the initial "breath of fresh air" reaction. Instead, the media had to be convinced that they should treat him seriously, something they learned slowly as Ventura dominated the debates and rose in the polls. The media happily reported when they had a "scoop" on Jesse as not being as stupid as you might think, or that he was mobbed by people who saw him as "plain-spoken" and genuine, but they passed over the initial burst of kindness toward him and instead accorded a long initial period of bemused reporting on this former wrestler who was running for governor and the surprising response people were giving him. By the time the media entered the usual first stage of kindness to a third-party contender, the race was almost over and there was little time to scrutinize his lack of experience or firm policy proposals. Only a few hurried editorials at the end of the race raised these questions. (For a quantified examination of this trend, see Appendix B.)

The fortuity of the media viewing Ventura as an amusing sideshow, but one whose candidacy they were professionally bound to cover with a measure of constancy and credibility, is arguably unique to this time and this person. Ventura is famous for wearing feather boas and for fake fighting. The source of attraction to the surreal feature of the American cultural landscape that is professional wrestlers escapes many people. In defense of the reporters, then, it would be hard not to be influenced in the direction of general amusement when one of them wants to be governor. A celebrity of another stripe—an athlete or an actor, for instance—would not be so comical and so easy to leave alone except for constant references to what they did in their former life. And so, as strange and counterintuitive as it may seem, Jesse "The Body" actually helped Jesse "The Mind" get his amateur-political-candidate self under the news media's radar for a long time, suddenly emerging as the straight-talking, common-sense Everyman right before the general election. There was just enough perfunctory treatment of him early on and through most of the race for people to learn what a good guy he was and how down-to-earth his ideas were while hardly ever raising issues of his readiness to serve as governor. In other words, and without deigning to pass judgment on anyone, the press ultimately provided little reason to the citizens of Minnesota as to why they should not vote for Jesse Ventura for governor.

Analysis of the Media's Treatment of Ventura

A content analysis–based investigation into how the news media behaved during the race shows a very positive depiction of Jesse Ventura as a man and as a candidate, with very little scrutiny directed his way—all of which is even more stark when compared to their treatment of Norm Coleman and Skip Humphrey. Data for this analysis was taken mainly from the state's two major newspapers, the Minneapolis *Star Tribune* (circulation 343,729) and the *St. Paul Pioneer Press* (circulation 207,624).[110] The analysis was done by compiling all the articles on the election, taking a random sample, and conducting a formal content analysis (see Appendix C).

Television news coverage also was considered, though only qualitatively, to corroborate and illustrate the quantitative analysis of the newspaper reporting. Also, a request for the military service record of Jesse Ventura was filed (possible under the Freedom of Information Act), and its results suggest that the media may have ignored a hole in his credibility.[111]

The Creation of the Ventura Mystique

Though for most people the backdrop of Ventura's candidacy was his status as a professional wrestler, his campaign wanted his having been a U.S. Navy SEAL to be the focal point, not only because it is impressive but also to counteract a certain perception of lack of depth on his part. The claim that James Janos (alias Jesse Ventura) was a SEAL, however, is suspicious to anyone bothering to do some simple research. Ventura's service record indicates that he did in fact graduate from BUD/S (Basic Underwater Demolition School), which is the first (and hardest) step in SEAL training.[112] However, whether Ventura became a SEAL is another matter. According to his record, he served in UDT 12 (Underwater Demolition Team Twelve), an assignment decidedly different than being on a SEAL team. A UDT member is essentially a frogman, schooled in diving and demolitions (for blowing up underwater obstacles before amphibious assaults, for example). Most telling, Ventura's records do not indicate that he was ever awarded the Seal Trident.

It is specious for Ventura to sell himself as a former SEAL because it implies much more in most people's minds than what he actually did in the navy. It is even more inaccurate to sell himself as a Vietnam veteran. According to his records, he did earn the Vietnam Service Medal. However, that is given out for service in "contiguous waters."[113] His records do not indicate that he was awarded the RVN Vietnam Campaign Ribbon. According to an e-mail written by the head of a SEAL fraternity, Ventura spent his time on an amphibious assault craft off the coast of South Vietnam.[114] Ventura did not earn a Combat Action Ribbon, according to his records, when at the time all SEALs were trained specifically for jungle warfare and sent to Vietnam, where they engaged in some of the most serious fighting of the war. If Ventura were really a navy SEAL, he would have been sent to Vietnam and engaged in the battles they fought; any reporter could have asked him during the campaign why he did not earn a combat ribbon and thus found out the truth.[115]

Sometime after the election, various individuals began pointing this out. A former SEAL in San Diego wrote a newspaper column about Ventura in which he highlighted the important distinction between serving on a UDT and what it means to be a SEAL, especially during Vietnam. Public radio did a story on the issue, as did some other news outlets, but it more or less passed without much attention (partly because of successful damage control on the part of the Ventura administration, partly because of the nuance of the point), leaving one to wonder if the reaction would have been different during the election, when it mattered.

An Absence of Scrutiny

During the entire campaign, the press never bothered to investigate Ventura's background. This sort of absence of scrutiny characterized much of his press coverage. His lack of government experience, his secretly harbored dream of legalized prostitution and drugs, his absence of policy plans—all these things were given only slight attention by the media (see Figure C.4 in Appendix C).

Related to this, there was throughout the campaign a portrayal in the press of Ventura as "the better guy." Content analysis provides a good sense of how much of the coverage in the two major newspapers that involved personal qualities featured Coleman and Humphrey's bad qualities—their meanness, poor leadership, fecklessness, and just about anything else that cast them in a poor light. Compare this to the positive image offered of Ventura—of honesty, of being a "regular guy," of being above politics.[116] As an example, take the ABC-affiliate's evening news story on last-minute campaigning that aired October 30, 1998. First was a segment on Skip Humphrey's visit from, of all people, Hillary Clinton, and in tandem they beat the dead horse of Skip's same old message (more programs to help more children). Following this was Norm Coleman in Duluth, giving yet another speech about tax cuts and "growth and opportunity." The last spot was on Jesse's Drive to Victory and the surprising turnout he was getting at his stops along the way; furthermore, whereas neither Norm nor Skip's spots had people commenting on why they liked them—other than Hillary Clinton—there was a teenage girl saying about Jesse, "He stands up for what he believes in, no matter what anybody says." As Ventura dismounts his RV wearing a Timberwolves jacket, an older man holding a Ventura sign says, "Look at this guy. Not a professional politician. A citizen politician."[117]

To be fair, Coleman and Humphrey both did plenty to look like a couple of petty politicians trying to win at all costs, flip-flopping on issues, running nothing other than the same, droning cacophony of ads, bickering at the debates, and accusing each other of everything from lying to hating family farms—while Ventura sat back, shaking his head, periodically adding things like, "Well, I think it shows obviously who's above all of this."

But Ventura was as guilty of being a flip-flopper as Coleman on guns or Humphrey on gay marriage. At the beginning of the race, he promised to cut taxes, but during the debates, pressed on his lack of a budget plan, he insisted that he was refusing to make promises that could be irresponsible—the only thing he would promise to do was to return the tax surplus to the taxpayers. Whether or not returning the surplus is on a philosophical level tantamount to a tax cut, his dual claims—that he would give back the entire surplus and that a promise to cut taxes no matter what was irresponsible—seem contradictory. Considering that the fate of the surplus and the tax system were probably more central to the future of the state than gay marriages or concealed weapon permits, it seems that pointing out Ventura's inconsistencies might have been warranted. But nobody—not the media, not his opponents—called him on it. The media never even pointed out in their stories about Ventura, in which he often cited a $4 billion tax surplus that he waved around like a battle flag (as he described it, $1,000 for each person in the state), that there was no $4 billion tax surplus. Former Governor Carlson was almost incredulous at this, saying, "Ventura kept running around saying that there was a $4 billion surplus and that he would return it. This was totally untrue. Never in the history of the State of Minnesota did we have a $4 billion surplus. But again, nobody, including the media, challenged him."[118] The actual size of the surplus at the beginning of February 1998—the time when Ventura said the state had a $4 billion surplus—was $2.1 billion.[119]

Another good example is Ventura's obvious hope to legalize drugs and prostitution. He repeatedly made public comments to that effect and suggested that the state should tax marijuana users. But the media made almost no mention of it; there were no articles, no editorials against him. As was mentioned, he was asked about it during a debate, but he dismissed it as a rumor started by the media. Ventura's plans for governing were decidedly more nebulous than Coleman's and Humphrey's. But the press did not question him about his plans. There was no story entitled "Ventura Fails to Deliver Budget Plan" or "Reform Party Candidate Refuses to Answer Questions on Education." Nobody asked him why he did not have an answer, whether he thought he should know, or when he might find out.[120]

The issue of gay marriage is yet another example of the media's lack of scrutiny when it came to Jesse Ventura. The *Star Tribune* ran a story on the subject on October 24 that had Coleman and the Republicans accusing Humphrey of supporting same-sex marriage; and Humphrey, who had said in an earlier interview that he would support the practice, denying that; and in turn Coleman accusing Humphrey of flip-flopping and Humphrey accusing Coleman of hate-mongering.[121] Nowhere in the story was Ventura mentioned. This explosive issue passed him by, with the other two candidates and the news media ignoring him. Although it may be to someone's advantage to be on this side or that of an issue in a very public way, in doing so one also loses at least some support. Not so Ventura. Asked about gay marriage during a debate, both Norm and Skip gave their company lines, but Jesse, without being forced to admit whether he supported it or not, told a story about his two gay friends who cannot visit each other when one of them is in the hospital. He concludes by saying, "Government shouldn't be so mean. Love is bigger than government." This seemingly most hetero-sexual man on the planet was, as is apparent, able to walk the line per-fectly, appealing both to angry white males and gay people, becoming in the process all things to all people.

Even at the very end of the campaign, when it occurred to people that he might win, the press could hardly stop talking about his rising poll numbers and his appeal to voters. There was something amounting to a hard look at the man for whom so many people wanted to vote on October 31, titled "Would Gov. Ventura Be Able to Govern Effectively? Political Observers Disagree." The gist of the article was that it would be fine if Jesse Ventura were elected. His lack of allies in the legislature (something Ventura played to his advantage by telling people that good government is divided government), not his paucity of experience in government or his poor knowledge of the philosophical underpinnings of a democratic society, was the seeming focus of the piece, which men-tioned that even Governor Carlson concurred with several respected state legislators, including the only official independent, that Ventura would be able to form effective coalitions with Republicans and Democrats.

Even when Ventura suggested the legalization of prostitution, the press gave him a boost. Nick Coleman wrote a column in the *Pioneer Press* a few days after the incident entitled, "Ventura's Straight Talk Merits Respect." He wrote that Ventura had "committed a cardinal sin in politics: He dared to think out loud."[122] Thus, something that might have sunk Humphrey or Coleman in a straight-laced place like Min-nesota became another "antipolitics" positive for Ventura.

And then, despite having endorsed Coleman, the *Pioneer Press* of-fered a sort of bizarre endorsement of Ventura on November 1. It ran an elaborate multipage story with several photos from Minnesota poli-tics of days past with the headline "In the First Half of the 20th Century, Three Popular Governors Have Struck the Reformist Themes that Have Dominated Minnesota Politics Ever Since."[123]

A few days earlier, an article appeared in the same paper with the headline "Ventura Ready to Beat the Odds." Focusing on a Ventura speech at a local Kiwanis Club luncheon, the writer admits that "through-out the campaign, Ventura has gotten away with presenting far sketchier policy proposals than his rivals," but then lays the blame on his rivals: "Coleman and Humphrey have battled each other over the level of de-tail in their tax-and-spending plan, but neither has seriously criticized

Ventura for promising a budget plan and failing to deliver."[124] This reads a bit like clarity finally creeping in, albeit a bit late.

Summary

Ventura's win is commonly explained as a fluke event of celebrity. But the analysis here shows that the fact that Ventura was a celebrity running *in Minnesota* is the far more important reason for his win. Unusual electoral rules in Minnesota helped Ventura overcome the barriers that typically punish a third party's effort. He automatically appeared on the ballot and thus did not have to spend time and money gathering signatures. Indeed, because of Minnesota's rules, he was listed first on the ballot, just as sports teams with the worst records in the most recent season get first round draft picks. Ventura was automatically included in the debates, which conferred legitimacy and credibility that third-party candidacies usually lack, and it was at this time that his poll numbers began to rise. And because the other candidates attacked each other savagely during the debates, Ventura benefited by appearing to rise above politics as usual. Finally, Ventura received through generous state campaign finance laws over $300,000 that he used to buy television advertising time. Though the other candidates spent more, Ventura's allotment was enough to mount a credible campaign, particularly because the campaign concentrated on the Twin Cities media market and did not waste money on outlying areas.

Thus Ventura won not because he was a celebrity but because he was running in Minnesota. Ventura's celebrity is relevant, though not in the way commentators and pundits have suggested. It was instead the *nature* of Ventura's celebrity, not so much the celebrity itself, that allowed him to sneak under the media's radar. It is fair to say that, on balance, the media did not take him as seriously as they might have and thus did not scrutinize his record, his statements, or his plan (or lack of one) for governing. Ventura experienced a media pattern the opposite of what most third parties encounter. Rather than enjoy an early honeymoon followed by decreasing and finally negative coverage, he was largely ignored and later recognized and even lauded. His media coverage was never prominently negative, and the media did not fixate on the "wasted vote" argument. Depending on how much one should properly view the media's role in shaping public opinion, it may be impossible to distinguish this reality from Ventura's victory itself.

As has been shown, the Reform Party ran a smarter, better campaign than their opponents, and the media coverage reflected that. Ventura is charismatic and intelligent, and almost everything he said was original. He got himself a lot of attention, and much of it was positive. But ultimately there was less scrutiny directed at him, especially compared to the harsh eye turned to Coleman and Humphrey and the years of public service they had given.

The usual barriers to success that greet most third parties in America were obviated here because of the unique structure of elections in Minnesota and because of how the media reacted to Ventura. With these barriers removed, or at least lessened considerably, he was able to run as a legitimate candidate—and be a protest candidate at the same time—co-opting a host of issues and strengths from each of the other two candidates. Still, Ventura would not have won had he not been able to get first-time voters out, again, specifically *in Minnesota*, where they could register on election day.

The election of Jesse Ventura came about because specific events intersected perfectly. People might try to sound smart by assigning responsibility this way or that, but the reality is that this election was the perfect intersection of institutions (same-day registration, public financing, automatic debate entrance) and personality (a celebrity with a type of charismatic appeal that brought new voters out to the polls while encouraging the media and his opponents to leave him alone). I have shown how it is possible to get a clear picture of which factors intersected—what mattered—and which did not (for instance, the votes of working-class people were far more important than those of young voters).

The source and nature of Ventura's triumph having thus been explicated, the discussion in the next chapter turns to what this all means for the field of political science.

Notes

1. See Federal Election Commission, "Frequently Asked Questions About Voter Registration and Voting." Available on the Internet at http://www.fec.gov/pages/faqs.htm.
2. This data was fortunately available in a computer readable file from the Minnesota Secretary of State's Office, Elections Division, *1998 State Primary Election and State General Election.*
3. The specific program used is an ecological inference computer program developed by Harvard University Professor Gary King known as EzI(.
4. Rick McCluhan, chairman of the Minnesota Reform Party, 24 July 1999, telephone interview by the author, Cambridge, MA, to Mankato, MN.

5. Bill Cooper, chairman of the Minnesota Republican Party, 3 September 1999, interview by the author, Wayzata, MN.

6. Mike Landy, Reform Party activist, 16 August 1999, telephone interview by the author, Mahtomedi, MN, to St. Cloud, MN.

7. Gene Franchett, Ventura campaign worker, 28 July 1999, telephone interview by the author, Cambridge, MA, to Minneapolis, MN.

8. At the 1999 Minnesota State Fair, one seventeen-year-old had this to say: "Man, it was like a revolution, and we all voted for our man Jesse."

9. Kathy Czar, former DFL executive director, 21 July 1999, telephone interview by the author, Cambridge, MA, to Minneapolis, MN.

10. My use of the term *dude* is not meant in any pejorative sense.

11. Kathy Czar interview, 21 July 1999.

12. This is not an exact category or a perfect picture of what a "dude" is, and $50,000 might be high as an upper level by which to define this group. Still, it is a satisfactory definition that goes far to capture their essential characteristics, as shown in the table that follows.

13. These groups are used for the purposes of comparison; they are not meant to suggest that they are "antidudes" or the polar opposite of that group.

14. These results would have been even more pronounced had I defined *dudes* as having income of $30,000 or less. Thus the results in Table 3.2 present a very conservative estimate of a "dude"-"nondude" difference.

15. Alan Shilepsky, former Reform Party candidate for Minnesota Secretary of State, 15 August 1999, telephone interview by the author, Mahtomedi, MN, to Minneapolis, MN.

16. Tony Carlson, DFL activist and Ventura volunteer, 20 July 1999, telephone interview by the author, Cambridge, MA, to Minneapolis, MN.

17. Jack Meeks, Republican National Committeeman from Minnesota, 17 August 1999, telephone interview by the author, Mahtomedi, MN, to St. Paul, MN.

18. If Coleman and Ventura had taken equally from this group (leaving Humphrey's take constant), the final result would have had Ventura winning, according to the exit poll, 36.2 to 35.8 percent; but, of course, exit polls are just a rough estimate, and Coleman might have won.

19. CNN.com, "Honesty Ranks First in Choosing Candidates," 30 November 1999.

20. Arne Carlson, 9 September 1999, interview by the author, Minneapolis, MN.

21. Rick McCluhan interview, 24 July 1999.

22. Alan Shilepsky interview, 15 August 1999.

23. Mavis Huddle, 28 July 1999, telephone interview by the author, Cambridge, MA, to Northfield, MN.

24. Kathy Czar interview, 21 July 1999.

25. Stephen Frank and Steven Wagner, *"We Shocked the World!" A Case Study of Jesse Ventura's Election as Governor of Minnesota* (Fort Worth: Harcourt College Publishers, 1999), p. 22.

26. Bob von Sternberg, 18 July 1999, telephone interview by the author, Cambridge, MA, to Minneapolis, MN.

27. This could be ascribed to the inaccuracies of exit polling (see Andrea L. Campbell and Bradley Palmquist, "Exit Polls as a Source of Political Data," *1998 Annual Meeting of the American Political Science Association* [Boston:

APSA, 1998]) or it could be that some farmers who voted for Coleman, in the midst of the farm crisis proposals to slash farm taxes, chose taxes as their most important issue.

28. The issues of concealed carry laws and public stadium financing are not depicted in Table 3.7 and were a separate question in the poll.

29. According to the VNS poll, Ventura pulled 44 percent of the self-described ideologically "liberal" vote, more than Humphrey's 42.2 percent. He won 38 percent of the moderate vote (more than either of the other two) and only 29 percent of the conservative vote.

30. See Steven J. Rosenstone, Roy L. Behr, and Edward H. Lazarus, *Third Parties in America* (Princeton: Princeton University Press, 1993).

31. State of Minnesota, Economic Resource Group, *1998 Economic Report to the Governor* (St. Paul: Offices of the Economic Resource Group, 1998), p. 3.

32. Ibid.

33. Ibid., p. 4.

34. Tom Gillaspy, state demographer, 21 June 2000, telephone conversation with the author, Cambridge, MA, to St. Paul, MN.

35. State of Minnesota, Minnesota Planning Agency, Criminal Justice Center, *Minnesota Homicides 1985–1997* (St. Paul: Minnesota Planning Agency, 1999), p. 6.

36. Ibid., p. 7.

37. State of Minnesota, Minnesota Planning Agency, Criminal Justice Center, *Judging by the Data: Offenders in Minnesota's Juvenile Courts* (St. Paul: Minnesota Planning Agency, 1999), p. 6.

38. State of Minnesota, Minnesota Planning Agency, Criminal Justice Center, *Reported Crimes 1985–1997* (St. Paul: Minnesota Planning Agency, 1999).

39. Frank and Wagner, *"We Shocked the World!"* p. 13.

40. "The Land of Good Lessons," *The Economist* 344 (5 July 1997), p. 28.

41. State of Minnesota, Minnesota Planning Agency, *1996 Children's Services Report Card* (St. Paul: Minnesota Planning Agency, 1996).

42. Minnesota Department of Children, Families, and Learning, 1999, as cited in Frank and Wagner, *"We Shocked the World!"* p. 13.

43. State of Minnesota, Minnesota Planning Agency, *1996 Children's Services Report Card*.

44. Frank and Wagner, *"We Shocked the World!"* p. 13.

45. Rosenstone, Behr, and Lazarus, *Third Parties in America,* p. 20.

46. Ibid.

47. Ibid., p. 21.

48. Ibid., p. 22.

49. J. David Gillespie, *Politics at the Periphery* (Columbia: University of South Carolina Press, 1993), p. 36.

50. Rosenstone, Behr, and Lazarus, *Third Parties in America,* p. 30.

51. Other states have similar rules, and of course there is a galactic difference between getting on the ballot in a single state for a run for governor and getting on the ballot in fifty states for a presidential campaign, so this is perhaps not the most significant of all of Minnesota's different rules, but it's still one less thing the Reform Party has to deal with.

52. Dean Barkley interview, 3 August 1999.

53. Jeanne Olson, executive director of the Campaign Finance and Public Disclosure Board, 24 February 1999, telephone conversation with the author, Cambridge, MA, to St. Paul, MN.

54. Gillespie, *Politics at the Periphery,* pp. 32–33.

55. Ibid., pp. 9–12.

56. Rosenstone, Behr and Lazarus, *Third Parties in America,* p. 30.

57. Ibid.

58. Daniel Elazar, Virginia Gray, and Wyman Spano, *Minnesota Politics and Government* (Lincoln: University of Nebraska Press, 1999), p. 80.

59. Conversation with Jeanne Olson, 24 February 1999.

60. Elazar, Gray, and Spano, *Minnesota Politics and Government,* p. 80.

61. Ibid., p. 68.

62. Ibid., p. 83.

63. Gillespie, *Politics at the Periphery,* p. 31.

64. Rosenstone, Behr, and Lazarus, *Third Parties in America,* p. 26.

65. Gillespie, *Politics at the Periphery,* p. 32.

66. Rosenstone, Behr, and Lazarus, *Third Parties in America,* p. 26.

67. Ibid.

68. Thus, even a system that is open to new party challenges has legitimacy requirements, low though they may be.

69. Elazar, Gray, and Spano, *Minnesota Politics and Government,* p. 81.

70. Ibid.

71. Frank and Wagner, *"We Shocked the World!"* p. 27.

72. Elazar, Gray, and Spano, *Minnesota Politics and Government,* p. 81.

73. Conversation with Jeanne Olson, 24 February 1999.

74. State of Minnesota, Campaign Finance and Public Disclosure Board, "Minnesota's Public Subsidy Program," 1999. Published memorandum.

75. Conversation with Jeanne Olson, 24 February 1999.

76. Ibid.

77. State of Minnesota, Campaign Finance and Public Disclosure Board, *1998 Campaign Finance Summary* (St. Paul: Offices of the Campaign Finance and Public Disclosure Board, 1999), p. 1.

78. Conversation with Jeanne Olson, 24 February 1999.

79. Chris Georgacas, former chairman of the Republican Party of Minnesota and Coleman campaign manager, 4 August 1999, interview by the author, Maplewood, MN; Skip Humphrey, DFL nominee for governor and former attorney general of Minnesota, 12 August 1999, interview by the author, Bloomington, MN; Phil Madsen e-mail, 29 January 2000.

80. Frank and Wagner, *"We Shocked the World!"* p. 25.

81. Bill Hillsman, CEO of North Woods Advertising and Ventura campaign media consultant, 26 August 1999, interview by the author, Minneapolis, MN.

82. Frank and Wagner, *"We Shocked the World!"* p. 23.

83. Phil Madsen, 23 February 2000, *Re: Quick Questions* (e-mail note to the author).

84. Ibid.

85. Frank and Wagner, *"We Shocked the World!"* p. 23.

86. Bill Hillsman interview, 26 August 1999.

87. Frank and Wagner, *"We Shocked the World!"* p. 24.

88. Frank and Wagner, p. 25.

89. "Barkley: Ventura Campaign Has Dire Cash Woes," *St. Paul Pioneer Press,* 9 October 1998, p. 7C.

90. Frank and Wagner, *"We Shocked the World!"* p. 25.

91. Jesse Ventura, interview with the author, 6 October 1999, Cambridge, MA.

92. Gillespie, *Politics at the Periphery,* p. 33.

93. Rosenstone, Behr, and Lazarus, *Third Parties in America,* p. 35.

94. A candidate is automatically included if representing a legally defined major party (as Ventura was) but can also be included if polling about 5 percent in an "independent, credible, statewide, professional poll," or if they are receiving a percentage of support in a poll that is equal to or greater than that of a major party.

95. Sally Sawyer, executive director of the Minnesota League of Women Voters, 25 February 2000, telephone conversation with the author, Cambridge, MA, to St. Paul, MN.

96. Ibid., 28 August 2000, telephone conversation with the author, Mahtomedi, MN, to St. Paul, MN.

97. Rosenstone, Behr, and Lazarus, *Third Parties in America,* p. 118.

98. http://www.lwvmn.org/MNCompact/back.html.

99. Ibid.

100. Conversation with Sally Sawyer, 25 February 2000.

101. Rosenstone, Behr, and Lazarus, *Third Parties in America,* p. 35.

102. Ibid.

103. Bob von Sternberg interview, 18 July 1999.

104. Mike Freeman, 27 August 1999, interview with the author, Minneapolis, MN.

105. This data was gathered by performing a search on the Nexis-Lexis search engine.

106. Rosenstone, Behr, and Lazarus, *Third Parties in America,* p. 36.

107. Ibid., pp. 264–265.

108. Ibid., pp. 118 and 39–41.

109. Ibid., p. 41.

110. Elazar, Gray, and Spano, *Minnesota Politics and Government,* p. 85.

111. See Appendices.

112. National Personal Records Center. Service Record of James George Janos. St. Louis, MO.

113. Colonel John P. Gritz (USASF-Ret.), 27-year Army Special Forces officer, 16 August 1999, telephone conversation with the author, Mahtomedi, MN, to Eagan, MN.

114. Bob Rieve, 8 June 1999, executive director of SEAL of APPROVAL, e-mail to John Gritz *Re: Fw: Know a Good SEAL?*

115. Conversation with Colonel John P. Gritz, 16 August 1999.

116. Again, it is unfair to claim that the qualitative form of the press coverage is due entirely to some bias on the part of the media; reporters were in many ways reporting what *was* in fact going on in the campaign—Coleman and Humphrey bickering with each other while Ventura, ignored by his opponents,

charmed people with his amiable persona. The content analysis of the personal qualities and the governing abilities of the candidates should not be read simply as a sweeping indictment of the press corps.

117. KSTP-TV, St. Paul, "Last Minute Campaigning." Aired 31 October 1998.

118. Arne Carlson interview, 9 September 1999.

119. Charlie Bielick, director of budget planning, Minnesota Department of Finance, 9 March 2000, telephone conversation with the author, Cambridge, MA, to St. Paul, MN.

120. Bill Babcock, director of the Silha Center for the Study of Media Ethics and Law at the University of Minnesota, said in an August 16, 1999, interview that he was dismayed by the failure of the Twin Cities media to cover Ventura. He drew a comparison to David Duke's run for Congress in Louisiana, when the local newspaper editor covered Duke "like a hurricane" in a way absent of any bias but that investigated and exposed the truth of his life. While in no way suggesting that Ventura is anything like David Duke, Babcock does think that the media had an added responsibility to get people "up to date" on him so that they could make completely informed voting decisions, especially since Minnesotans had sixteen years of experience with Skip Humphrey and five with Norm Coleman. It was the media's responsibility to make sure that voters knew as much about Ventura as they did about Humphrey and Coleman, and in Babcock's view they failed to deliver.

121. Patricia Lopez-Baden, "Candidates Trade Volleys in Dispute on Gay Marriage," Minneapolis *Star Tribune,* 24 October 1998, p. 1B.

122. Nick Coleman, "Ventura's Straight Talk Merits Respect," *St. Paul Pioneer Press,* 26 October 1998, p. 1C.

123. D. J. Tice, "Great Governors," *St. Paul Pioneer Press,* 1 November 1998, p. 1G.

124. "Ventura Ready to Beat the Odds," *St. Paul Pioneer Press,* 28 October 1998, p. 1C.

4

LESSONS FOR POLITICAL SCIENCE

Three aspects of Jesse Ventura's election invite investigation from the perspective of political theory. The first is that Ventura won running essentially as a celebrity candidate. Second is that a great number of people who had not voted before and had not cared to vote before came to the polls and voted for Ventura. Third, and this is perhaps most important, is that Ventura won this election while running as a candidate of a third party.

Celebrity Politics

"People have been looking at the new money since the war in economic terms only. Nobody will even take a look at our incredible new national pastimes, things like stock car racing, drag racing, demolition derbies, sports that attract five to ten million more spectators than football, baseball and basketball each year. Part of it is a built-in class bias. The educated classes in this country, as in every country, the people who grow up to control visual and printed communication media, are all plugged into what is, when one gets down to it, an ancient, aristocratic aesthetic. Stock car racing, custom cars—and, for that matter, the jerk, the monkey, rock music—still seem beneath serious consideration, still the preserve of ratty people with ratty hair and dermatitis and corroded thoracic boxes and so forth. Yet all these rancid people are creating new styles all the time and changing the life of the whole country in ways that nobody even seems to bother to record, much less analyze."
—Tom Wolfe, *The Kandy-Kolored Tangerine-Flake Streamline Baby*[1]

Many people have assumed that Jesse Ventura won the election because he is a celebrity, case closed. According to this view, his election is something of a fluke; this sort of thinking probably goes a long way toward explaining the paucity of academic inquiry. But his victory, as was shown in the previous chapter, is explained much more by Minnesota's unique electoral process than by his being a celebrity. It is, in fact, possible to isolate a pure "celebrity advantage," and it is indeed fairly low. First, Ventura's early polling numbers, which were taken before his campaign effectively began and which therefore measure his celebrity appeal qua celebrity appeal, never got above 10 percent (and this does not account for those people who would vote for a Reform Party candidate anyway, regardless of whether he or she were a celebrity). Moreover, Ventura's state fair appearance—which emphasized his celebrity-hood—had no effect on his polling numbers (see Appendix B, p. 138). It is fair to say, then, that Ventura's pure celebrity advantage—that is, the number of people willing to vote for him simply because he is famous—was rather small, probably somewhere less than 10 percent.

Indeed, David Canon, the author of *Actors, Athletes, and Astronauts*, pointed out that Ventura's celebrity advantage was handicapped by his alignment to a third party, since there was no traditional apparatus to set up fundraisers for ogling celebrity-challengers.[2] This is true, but were he part of the two-party system, it's doubtful that the sort of persons who are regular party donors would have been that interested in a fundraising event featuring a local semi-celebrity who once wore a feather boa for professional reasons. In other words, for these sorts of people Jesse Ventura would probably not have the same appeal as a John Glenn or Bill Bradley, whose status as cultural icons seems worth a heftier donation.

Instead, the specific nature of Ventura's celebrity was probably best utilized in a third-party challenge: a bad-boy, low-rent entertainer whose appeal eludes many, rebelling against the system. How could he have sold T-shirts with the words "Retaliate in '98" on them (raising $150,000) if he were associated with a national party—"the system"? The proletarian fundraising power that Ventura brought to his campaign is perhaps the most important way in which to think about this race through the lens of "celebrity politics"—not the more common assumption that Ventura won simply because he *was* a celebrity.

Part of Canon's argument in *Actors, Athletes, and Astronauts* is that celebrity politicians make good challengers to political incumbents in part because of their fundraising potential. The role of Ventura's celebrity in fundraising for his own campaign might compel an extension of Canon's theory that would see celebrities as potentially strong challengers to the two-party system as well.

Beyond fundraising, celebrity as it relates to third parties might be valuable for its own sake, which would represent another extension of Canon's theory. If a third party fields a celebrity as a candidate for office, a particular advantage lies in his or her ability to get attention. Ventura's pure "celebrity advantage" was rather small. There are in any election a certain number of people willing to vote for a third party for the sake of doing so, and another group who will vote for a celebrity for the sake of doing so. The total of these voters was, in Ventura's case— as represented by his poll numbers in the early part of the race—fairly small. But most everyone probably instinctively paid more attention to him than they usually would a standard third-party challenge. The media and the public were interested in watching what he did in the campaign in part because he was a celebrity; and, because Ventura already had, to a certain degree, their attention, he was more easily able to convince voters that he was a legitimate candidate, with better ideas than the other two. Celebrity can in a way help a third-party candidate "prime the pump" of public interest and affection. Governor Ventura himself has suggested that in the future, third parties would be better off fielding celebrities for office because, in his view, then nobody has to raise special interest money just to introduce themselves to voters.

Another part of the advantage conferred by Ventura's distinctive celebrity can be seen in how the media and his opponents treated him. His advantage was that of low expectations, the best leverage one can be given in any situation. In other words, because expectations of him were low—how could someone take *him* seriously?—the media and his opponents did not attack him, letting him skate by unscathed. Moreover, because of the associations many people make between professional wrestling and intelligence, they were pleasantly surprised when he spoke intelligently or pointed out some minutia of public policy. One Republican Party official grasped this quite clearly, saying in an interview, "The expectations for Jesse were so low, all he had to do was not look like a fool and the perception would be that he did great."[3]

Another implication for the study of celebrity politics might be considered in some way a warning as well. There are many people who do not grasp how a professional wrestler could have been elected governor of a state. In their minds professional wresting is a bizarre, low-end, bogus, unintelligent form of entertainment. For them, it is an aberration in society, an amusing sideshow of an eyesore on the American cultural landscape. They cannot see how achieving notoriety in a fake sport could ever be anything but a disadvantage in running for office. And they assume that everyone holds wrestling in the same contempt they do.

But these people fail to realize that for a great number of Americans, professional wrestling is a perfectly legitimate form of culture. It is simply how they choose to spend their entertainment dollar, and it does not strike them as anything weird or bad or ironically amusing. The sort of self-assured, unthinking thinking that assumes the universal acknowledgment of pro wrestling's low status is similar to that of a politician who purposely speaks vaguely and feigns interest in everything in an effort to avoid offending anyone at all, never for a moment considering that there are probably a lot of people who would like a politician who did the opposite, who lost his temper and swore at people and challenged reporters to fights. When Ventura plaintively describes professional wrestling as "ballet with violence,"[4] he is not justifying it to the scores of millions of Americans to whom professional wrestling is perfectly legitimate culture—it is for those whose lives are disconnected from it and who he knows do not even pretend to understand. The disconnect between what the cultural elite appreciate and what for much of the rest of the country is real and important is something members of the former struggle to comprehend, which is something that irritates the latter. The person who grows up in Manhattan, attends Harvard, and then commutes from Connecticut back to a job in Manhattan is likely to look with scornful confusion at the American expanse that lies between New York and Los Angeles, and this bears itself out as a central aesthetic of the elite media. This gap is the one between those who live in the hip part of town, read the *New Yorker,* drink water out of a bottle, worry about being on top of things, and have inflated opinions of their own importance, and those who live in the suburbs and the country, drink Budweiser, hunt and fish, go to church on Sundays, and are uninterested in each new fad. The space between these two cultures in America is perhaps one of the least understood features of the cultural landscape, but it is one of the most important.

More pointedly, the fact of that matter is that, no matter how they might try, just because someone does not understand something does not make it less real, and dismissing certain political candidates out of hand because of their comical biographies, as to varying degrees the news media and the Republican and Democratic parties did in this election, assumes that the electorate dismisses them as well—an assumption that reflects equal parts arrogance and foolishness.

So it's not the case that Ventura won simply because he was a celebrity. It's not that people came out to vote for Jesse Ventura the wrestler and radio host. Voters are not fools. However, the impact of Ventura's celebrity was real, in several ways, and it is reasonable to believe that another person, someone without the same persona, would not have won the election.

Voting Theory

That Ventura won by getting what were then nonvoters to vote on election day invites reconsideration of aspects of voting theory. As was mentioned earlier, Minnesota is one of seven states with same-day voter registration laws.[5] In the last week of the race, Secretary of State Joan Growe predicted that turnout would be 53 percent, or just under 1.83 million voters. After the dust settled, turnout was over 61 percent, with over 2.1 million votes cast. Fully 332,540 people registered and voted for the first time on election day 1998.[6] Some polling stations had so many people showing up to vote that they ran out of ballots.

Without the voters who came out to register on election day, Ventura could not have won. First-time voters powered his victory. Sixty-nine percent of those same-day registrants voted for Ventura, which is just under 11 percent of the total electorate (Ventura won with 37 percent).[7]

Those who came out to vote for the first time were on average less-educated than other voters. Rosenstone and Wolfinger found in their seminal work *Who Votes?* that education level is the single most robust variable in predicting voting.[8] Those with more education have a much higher rate of voter turnout. Broadly, there are two sets of reasons cited by scholars. The first flows from the understanding of registering to vote as a "cost" in terms of time and energy; education, it is believed, reduces the costs associated with registering and voting by schooling one in the ways of bureaucracies and form-filing, increasing the "ability to handle the humdrum bureaucratic requirements of registering and voting."[9]

The second set of reasons generally cited for higher turnout among the more educated looks at the motivation to vote, the "benefit" side of taking part in democracy. In addition to enabling one to more easily overcome the barriers, or costs, to voting, education, it is argued, intensifies one's sense of the benefits of voting, teaching a student to see the long-term connection between a vote cast today and the probable effects on their lives tomorrow. Rosenstone and Wolfinger write, "Schooling increases one's capacity for understanding and working with complex, abstract, and intangible subjects, that is, subjects like politics."[10] Sidney Verba believes an education imparts in people a sense that one can affect the system and, in addition, that one has a duty to vote.

Current voting theory touches on both motivation and the costs of voting. Thus the significance of education for turnout may be in reducing the bureaucratic registrant hurdle (the cost), or it may be in imparting in people a sense of civic duty (the benefit). The unique intersection of Minnesota's voting rules and Ventura's presence in this race offers an opportunity to adjudicate between these two factors.

Political scientist Ben Highton compared turnout in North Dakota, which has no registration requirement, with turnout in the rest of the United States. If the significance of education to turnout were solely as an aid to overcoming the registration hurdle, then within the state of North Dakota, turnout of the less educated should equal that of the more educated. What he found, however, is that in North Dakota there are still differences in turnout rate by education level; in other words, even when there is no registration hurdle, the less educated are less likely to vote than the more educated. He concludes that education matters to turnout as a motivational force as well.[11]

The 1998 Minnesota gubernatorial race permits a different test of the same proposition. By comparing North Dakota with the rest of the United States, Highton assessed the impact of differing levels of registration hurdles. A comparison of Minnesota turnout by education level in 1998 with that of 1990 and 1994 allows us to assess the effect of different *motivation* levels. The registration hurdle was the same low election-day registration (requiring just a driver's license or a neighbor vouching for your residency) in all three years, but in 1998, the level of motivation was different: Jesse Ventura was running.

According to the 1990 Voter News Service (VNS) exit poll, 32 percent of those who voted had a high school education or less. In that election, 1,843,104 people voted.[12] This means that of these voters, approximately 589,800 were in the group having a high school education or less. In 1994, the VNS poll found that 29.2 percent of those who voted had a high school diploma or less. Of the 1,794,618 people who voted that year, about 524,000 were in this group. According to VNS, 31.4 percent of those who voted in 1998 had a high school education or less. Because turnout was up to 2,105,377, the number of voters who fell into this group was 661,088. This is an increase in low education voters of 12 percent over 1990 and 26 percent over 1994.[13]

Why the sudden turnout among the less-educated members of the electorate? The difference between the elections, of course, was Jesse Ventura. As longtime DFL activist Mary McEvoy put it, "Politics had never caught their attention, and Jesse caught their attention."[14]

Using this data, then, it is possible to adjudicate the relative importance of the sets of reasons used to explain why less-educated people vote less: bureaucratic hurdles ("costs") and motivation ("benefit"). When the bureaucratic hurdle was held constant but the level of motivation was increased with a Ventura candidacy, turnout among less-educated adults increased. Thus a significant portion of the importance of education to voting is motivating, not merely a bureaucratic barrier-reducer. It may be true that this jump would not have occurred if Minnesota had stricter, in-advance registration requirements, but it was clearly dependent on Ventura's ability to motivate voters.

As for why people of differing education levels vote at different rates, there is something to be said for the motivation of educated people to vote because they are voting for other educated people. The fact is, most politicians more closely resemble the educated than the less educated. Educated individuals may see a bit of themselves in the persons running for office. After all, they often have in common the shared experience of higher education. Less-educated people, in contrast, do not see themselves in most of their choices. Educated people may see in the lawyer-politician for whom they are voting clear similarities to themselves. The less educated, who may naturally feel some resentment toward the other group, do not feel this connection with candidates; they may, in fact, even feel alienated from them.

But in a man like Ventura, who himself does not have much formal education, who has working-class roots, who was a member of a union, and who served in the military, they can more easily see themselves and form a bond. As someone at one of Ventura's rallies yelled out, "Jesse, you are us!"[15]

This explanation as a reason for why less-educated people vote less regularly—that they just do not have as much in common with the candidates as more educated people do—has been missed by current theory. It is surely not the sole cause of lower turnout among those with less education, but it probably plays some role, as this group's gravitation to Ventura suggests.

Young people are another group the evidence points to as having a significant number of same-day registrants.[16] If we look at the VNS exit polls yet again, we see a similar finding. In 1990, 16.3 percent of the electorate was in the age group of 18 to 29, which translates to 300,425 voters. In 1994 the same age group was 14.2 percent of the electorate, translating to 254,836 voters. In 1998, the same age group made up 16.6 percent of the electorate, which is 349,493 voters, a 16 percent rise over

1990 and a 37 percent increase over 1994. The difference, again, was Ventura. As a college student said on a TV newscast on election day, "I came out to vote today strictly because of Jesse Ventura." Added his friend, "You gotta love the commercial with the action figures."[17]

Ruy Teixeira in *Why Americans Don't Vote* gives three general reasons for higher turnout among older people than among younger ones.[18] The first is the habit of doing so. Second, older people tend not to move around as much, making registering more worthwhile (because they will probably be around for the next few elections, unlike highly mobile young people). The third is a sense of a "stake in the system."

However, as Jesse Ventura's election demonstrates, it is entirely possible for an individual candidate to give young people a sense of a "stake in the system," even if they do not normally have one.

Third-Party Theory

Ventura's victory not only offers insight into how political science understands celebrity politics and voting but also sheds light on several aspects of third-party theory as well. This case is a good one for gaining ground in understanding third parties because of Minnesota's unique electoral rules and the large amount of data available for analysis.

Third, Ephemeral Parties

Despite many people's dislike for the two major parties and some people's yearning for a multiparty system, the plurality system (not to mention the electoral college at the national level) is perforce discriminatory against third parties. Unlike a parliamentary system that awards seats proportionally, the American system gives any office to the plurality-winner in that race alone; and so in a setting with three standing parties, the incentive is for the two parties whose ideologies are most similar to negotiate their differences, join together, and defeat the remaining party, as the Democrats and Farmer-Laborites did in Minnesota in the early 1940s. The object is to get more votes than one's competitor in any given contest; there is no trophy for second place in the American system. The system thus naturally supports two parties. This has the beneficial effect that most elected officials in the United States win with a majority of the vote, and it also simplifies decisionmaking for voters (who only have to decide between two parties). But there is also a tension between (1) the fact that the most efficient structure and therefore the natural paradigm is the two-party system, and (2) the reality that there is a great spectrum of interest and belief that must be satisfied by the two parties.

As Rosenstone, Behr, and Lazarus point out, most third-party candidacies have the effect of steering the debate, at least until their issues are co-opted by the two major parties.[19] This single member–simple plurality (SMSP) electoral system discriminates against third parties, and major parties can subvert them by co-opting their issues (for instance, after Ross Perot made the national deficit an issue in 1992, both major parties adopted deficit-reduction as an issue, leading some to wonder for what the Reform Party now stands). But during the times when they exist side by side with the two major parties, third parties can sometimes win elections, as Minnesota's governor demonstrated.

The Importance of Rules

There are two sets of reasons why third parties are condemned to the margins of politics in America. First are the inherent barriers of the U.S. plurality system, discussed in the preceding section. Those barriers are compounded by other conditions that favor the established parties and hinder third parties: ballot restrictions, limited financial resources, exclusion from debates, lack of press coverage, and voter and media antipathy to nonmajor party challengers.

It is this second set of conditions that Minnesota's unique brand of politics alleviates. Each of the problems traditionally plaguing third parties, but not inherent to the system in the way the plurality obstacle is, was overcome by the structure of Minnesotan political institutions. In 1998, even the state's media felt compelled to honor the Reform Party's legal major-party status with some attention.

It seems most obvious to conclude that the rules by which the game is played and the electoral structure in which parties operate are far more important to the success or failure of third-party bids than is celebrity. Rules do matter.

That these rules helped Ventura win the election is beyond doubt. But they also suggest something else. Perhaps the most startling reality of the election is that a third party in the Elysian fields of positive social and economic conditions outperformed the two major parties. The conditions under which the game was played were simply leveled, at least partially, by Minnesota's electoral rules, and once that was done, Ventura beat the other candidates fair and square.

Of course, according legal major-party status to any party that wins over 5 percent of the vote in an election and using this as a reason to necessarily include them in the debates and finance their campaign is not a birthright of any political party in the United States. Further, not allowing this is not necessarily wrong or unfair. However, the Minnesota example points to the possibility that politics in the United States could have a very different look—and radically different election outcomes—if Minnesota-type rules were the norm.

"Legitimacy" and the Reality of Perceptions

Another lesson the Ventura election holds for third-party theory is that perceptions matter. The "wasted vote" is an entirely psychological event, its underpinning argument rather circular: Voters decide that a candidate cannot win because nobody else will vote for him or her, so why "waste" their vote on a lost cause? It is a self-defeating event and relies on a sort of collective action problem—you cannot count on anyone else to vote for a third-party candidate, no matter how attractive, and so you decide not to do so either. It is all a matter of perception that rests on whether or not people see a candidate as being able to win. In this regard, the whole phenomenon is rather arbitrary.

Even when three parties do exist in relative parity in an election, there is still a legitimacy problem that needs to be overcome by the third party. As the Minnesota gubernatorial election shows, institutional rules confer this legitimacy with "legitimacy markers."

Consider the state fair and the debates. Ventura had an opportunity to exercise his considerable charm and charisma in retail politicking from his booth, with the potential to meet the 34 percent of Minnesotans who attended the fair. By all accounts, he and his booth were thoroughly popular with fairgoers. A local TV station sent out a crew to do a story on the Ventura booth, and state fair employees from the information booth told the campaign that his was the most asked-about booth of all.[20]

Given this exposure and the opportunity to function on Ventura's best level, one-on-one with citizens, we might expect his poll numbers to benefit. However, we can see in Appendix B (page 138) that, in fact, his numbers did not rise during or immediately after the fair. In fact, they do not begin to rise until the debates. They rise even more steeply when his commercials come on the air. All this points to the psychological nature of electoral "legitimacy." Usually, someone running for office from a third party battles for exposure. But not Ventura at the state fair. He enjoyed exposure and media attention. However, just about every minor party and marginal political activist group also had a booth. People know that it is easy and cheap to rent a state fair booth. It is, in short, unimpressive.[21] A booth at the fair is not—was not—a stamp of legitimacy.

Instead, Ventura's numbers went up after he appeared on TV as a major party candidate with Norm Coleman and Skip Humphrey. This suggests that people deem a candidate legitimate and potentially worthy of their vote when they see the candidate doing things that "real" candidates do. The same can be said for the effect of Ventura's TV commercials. A good part of their benefit was demonstrating to people that he was as much a "real" candidate as the other two. Airing TV commercials and debating with the major party candidates are legitimacy markers, and the candidate's poll numbers benefit.

The other way in which perceptions matter is how the media treats candidates from third parties. The Twin Cities media spent much time telling people that Ventura could not win the election. Then, in the last weeks of the campaign, the media increasingly announced his legitimacy as a contender (see Figure C.1, p. 142). Moreover, as has been shown, the media did not follow their usual pattern of third-party bids—an early embrace of the "outsider" message followed by a rejection of the candidate and a dismissal of his chances of actually winning. In Ventura's case, this pattern was reversed, partly because of his status as a former wrestler. The media dismissed him at first but then later conferred legitimacy and actually downplayed the "wasted vote" argument by announcing that he might well win the election. The media appears to have the ability to confer legitimacy or take it away. Governor Carlson says of the Fourth Estate, "The media has an awesome power. They decide, for example, who participates in the debates. And all too often they decide right and wrong and guilty and innocent. They have polls, polls, polls, every half-hour. They focus on who's ahead and who can win and less on issues. It's very shallow."[22] Regardless of its worth, though, the media's presentation of a candidate, as the Ventura case shows, can confer legitimacy—and take it away. For example, it is an interesting intellectual exercise to imagine what the 1992 presidential election might have looked like if Ross Perot were throughout the race accorded the same sort of laudatory attention given to, say, John McCain in the 2000 primary season.

Because voting for a third party involves stepping outside of the system—"an extraordinary act," Rosenstone, Behr, and Lazarus call it—it takes less to crush their supporters' faith.[23] And the media can do so with a degree of impunity. If they turn against a candidacy, it is doomed. But if they prop it up, the candidacy has at least a chance to succeed. Reform Party Minnesota secretary of state candidate Alan Shilepsky understood this election—and the form by which in politics reality follows perception—when he said, "They created the perception that this was real, and in the end, it was."[24]

The Future Hopes of Minor Parties

Rosenstone, Behr, and Lazarus, writing in *Third Parties in America* even before the advent of the Internet, suggest that technological advances might hold hope for third parties: "Finally, technological changes have allowed for increasingly sophisticated political strategies all without the aid of a political party. Independent-minded politicians who were once unwilling to embark on third-party campaigns without the help of an already existing locally based party can now take the plunge more readily."[25] This is only partially true.

Technology does make campaigning cheaper and doing so without a party apparatus easier. The Ventura campaign used the Internet to exhort people to register to vote, for example, and to coordinate the Drive to Victory. It is also fair to say that certain technological advances (e.g., television advertising) have come to be marks of legitimacy. But as the Ventura state fair experience shows, a campaign that does not have marks of legitimacy, as often conferred by the institutional arrangements in which it exists, will wither and die, no matter how large its e-mail address list.

This reality does not bode well for those who hold out hope for newfound third-party power in new technologies like the Internet. There are those who think that the low cost of web sites and the ease with which people can communicate to large audiences will put third parties in the hunt for some real victories. These hopes, however, are mistaken.

The Internet may allow a third party to overcome the exposure problem, just as the state fair did for Jesse Ventura. However, most people know that maintaining a web site is not expensive, and they know that it is not necessarily indicative of broad-based popular support. The Internet does not confer the legitimacy to overcome the wasted vote problem plaguing third parties: This is due, in large part, to the psychological effect on voters of the institutional structure in which parties operate.

Third Parties Reconsidered

Scholars of third parties in the United States have generally focused on two broad types of third parties. The first is the sort Rosenstone, Behr, and Lazarus discuss in *Third Parties in America*, the sort that arises when the two major parties are seen as failing to address some set of issues to the full satisfaction of a certain group. Such parties, like the

Greenbacks or the States' Rights Party, can broadly be grouped under the label of *splinter-secessionist third parties*. As the authors of *Third Parties* demonstrated, these parties have the primary effect of stealing votes from the two major parties and so can help direct the discourse of the race (the States' Rights Party, for instance, compelled both Harry Truman and Thomas Dewey to restrain their positions on civil rights for black Americans).[26] Ross Perot's United We Stand America quasi-party in the 1992 election fits this pattern as well, representing people who felt the two major parties were inadequate in addressing the national debt.

The second type of third party often discussed is what might be called the *ideological-doctrinaire* type. J. David Gillespie explicitly names this as a type (calling them "continuing doctrinal parties") in *Politics at the Periphery*.[27] Of this sort are the Socialist Workers Party, the American Nazi Party, the U.S. Taxpayers Party, and the Green Party.[28] These parties, Gillespie writes, usually prefer to be right than to win.[29] While these parties tend to lie, to varying degrees, at the outskirts of the nation's political life, they do serve the valuable function of affording people whose discontent with the current political order runs deep a peaceful outlet through which to "let off some steam" at the system and vent their dissatisfaction.[30]

The current state of third-party theory is inadequate to the task of fully understanding third parties in contemporary America. The two types of parties discussed above both exist, but there is in fact a third type of third party in America, one that is both recently emerged and predisposed to success in ways the other two types can never be.

In 1942 Wisconsin elected as governor Orlando Loomis of the Wisconsin Progressive Party. After this, there were essentially no third-party governors in the American states for almost fifty years (excepting Maine's 1974 election of Independent James Longley) until a string of third-party gubernatorial victories in the decade of the 1990s, beginning with Lowell Weicker of A Connecticut Party and Walter Hickel of the Alaska Independence Party.[31]

Following these two elections, the 1990s witnessed further third-party success with Angus King in Maine in 1994 and Jesse Ventura in 1998. The contention here is that these four victories, so close together after an amazingly long dry spell of third-party gubernatorial victories, are emblematic of a new and separate type of third party in the United States. In contrast to the other two types of third parties in modern America, this type has the political ability to win elections.

A reporter during the 1998 campaign asked Rosenstone, who is currently a dean at the University of Minnesota, about Ventura's candidacy.

He seemed to project his theory of third parties, which mostly concerns the splinter-secessionist type, and said, "The impact will be on the kinds of things candidates are forced to talk about."[32] Obviously, he was wrong, as Ventura is currently governor of Minnesota. Instead of belonging to the splinter-secessionist type of third party, Ventura belongs to a third type of third party whose salient characteristic, more than shaping discourse, is its ability to win elections outside the two-party system.

Groundwork for a New Theory of Third Parties in America

This type of third party can be described as a *pragmatic-utilitarian* type. As will be shown, all four of the contemporary third-party governors mentioned earlier share certain characteristics that can be identified as traits of the pragmatic-utilitarian type of third party. Admittedly, as there are only four examples from which to make conclusions, the following should be treated as the groundwork of a new theory and not as a complete or perfect law of political science.

Lowell Weicker was elected governor of Connecticut in 1990 when the then governor retired. A member of a prominent and wealthy Connecticut family, he had served as a well-regarded U.S. Senator for eighteen years as a Republican. As the economy slowed down in 1990 and the state faced a budget crisis, Weicker formed A Connecticut Party and entered the race. He was more famous than his rivals, Democratic Governor Bruce Morrison and Republican Congressman John Rowland. The state income tax was the central issue of the campaign, with Morrison in favor of it and Rowland strictly opposed to it. Weicker refused to rule it out, arguing that the far more responsible concern was for the state's budget. He led in the polls during the whole race, and he won with 40 percent of the vote.[33]

Walter Hickel won his election in Alaska with 39 percent of the vote. Hickel had served as governor as a Republican in the 1960s and then went on to be President Richard Nixon's Secretary of the Interior. He ran as a member of the Alaska Independence Party as a strong "boomer," someone more interested in economic development than in the environment.[34] He ran against the Democratic mayor of Anchorage, Tony Knowles, and Republican legislator Arliss Sturgulewski. Many Republicans considered Sturgulewski to be too liberal, and so they threw their support to Hickel.[35]

Hickel vowed to fight the federal government over control of Alaska's natural resources; his slogan "owner state" encompassed his philosophy of allowing Alaskans to determine for themselves what to do with the state's resources and promoting the state government's responsibility to ensure that they were used to the greatest benefit of the citizenry.[36] Both his opponents were to varying degrees environmentalists, something unpopular among many residents of the state.

Angus King ran as an independent in Maine in 1994. He had started his own energy conservation business and later sold it for $20 million. As host of a Maine Public Television show called *MaineWatch,* King began the campaign with a high degree of name recognition and, like Ventura, a familiarity with projecting his message on television.

King ran against former governor George Brennan, who had been governor in the 1970s; Susan Collins, who at the time was a former aide to outgoing governor John McKernan; and a Green Party candidate (in a similar fashion to the Minnesota Reform Party, the Green Party in Maine had maintained enough of a presence to be included in the debates).[37]

King was a social liberal (pro-choice and in favor of gay rights) and a fiscally conservative, pro-business candidate. In a state whose economy is constantly troubled and was beginning to recover from the recession of the early part of the decade, King presented himself as a commonsense businessman. He attacked high taxes and government waste, saying in a Ventura-like way that "Sometimes the best thing government can do is get out of the way."[38]

King also spent more than $1 million of his own money on the campaign, leading to a bitter series of attacks between himself and Brennan, who accused King of trying to buy the election.[39] He won with 35 percent of the vote to Brennan's 34 percent, a difference of less than 8,000 votes.[40]

Common Aspects

These nonmajor-party triumphs bear notable similarities. First, all four of the candidates were well-known in their states—Weicker and Hickel for previous government service, King and Ventura for their media careers. This suggests that when a candidate lacks a party label to get voters' attention, having name recognition helps to make up for the instinct of voters to ignore nonmajor parties; in other words, being well-known makes it easier for a third-party candidate to reach the elusive state of electoral legitimacy. Moreover, having a well-known person in the race running as a candidate of a third party is sure to generate far more press coverage than the typically unknown third-party candidate.

Another feature these four had in common was financial resources. Ventura, of course, had his public subsidy from the State of Minnesota, while King and Hickel were both millionaire entrepreneurs and financed their own campaigns. In other words, these men all had a way to overcome the financial barriers of running as a third-party candidate and reach a state of political legitimacy. In a similar way, both Hickel and Weicker also had support from many prominent members of their state's Republican Party who were unsatisfied with the party nominee.[41] (Ventura, too, had the support of disaffected Republicans and Democrats, but more among lower-level operatives.)

Moreover, they ran in states with but one major media market—in Minnesota, the Twin Cities; in Alaska, Anchorage; in Connecticut, Hartford; and in Maine, Portland (and to a lesser degree Bangor).[42] This makes sense: It is an easier task to propel a candidate running outside the major parties to the elusive, tenuous status of legitimacy through television exposure and advertising when it only has to be done *once*— not as regards money but in terms of convincing the collected voting populace that a candidate running outside the system *can* in fact win. This is easier when it's just *one* group of people talking to each other, agreeing that, hey, if you're going to vote for him then I might too, it could happen after all, don't-ya-know. It is, in other words, less difficult for a small or concentrated group of people (voters) to become convinced of someone's legitimacy than it is for a larger, more diverse, and more spread-out group to do the same.

The common features of these campaigns all have the same effect, which is to ease the burden of running as a member of a third party. Just as Minnesota's political playing field is particularly level because of its electoral rules, so too do other conditions affect the relative difficulty of a third-party bid.

Finally, it is interesting that none of the four governors ran against an incumbent officeholder. This is perhaps harder to tie to attaining legitimacy and how independent candidacies got it, but it might be argued that when an incumbent is running, voters can vote for or against him or her, but when an incumbent is not running, voters are compelled to take a harder look at the new candidates. In this circumstance, a third-party candidate might find it easier to get a look and run competitively against the two new major party candidates. In a similar way, it is interesting that in these elections the major party candidates were seen (to varying degrees) as unsatisfying choices; instead of looking at these victories as products of protest votes (which no doubt still existed), it might be more fair to say that in the context of what were seen as unsatisfying major party choices it was, in fact, easier for a third-party, independent candidate to get consideration from the voters (in other words, to give their candidacy legitimacy).

The Pragmatist-Utilitarian Third Party

This third type of third party is first and foremost pragmatic. Such parties do not have any sort of grand ideological vision for the country, the way ideological-doctrinaire third parties do, nor are they necessarily attached to any one hard-and-fast side of any one issue, the way splinter-secessionist types are. The pragmatic-utilitarian party instead presents itself as a sort of manager of the economic good and a fierce opponent of any constraining ideology that interferes with pragmatic decision-making. Common sense and realism are their buzzwords. Their candidates don't present grand visions of a utopian society when they run. Even Lowell Weicker, who had fought battles on principle (having taken on his own party during Watergate) and of whom it might reasonably be said that he pursued idealistic aims (the Americans with Disabilities Act) during his legislative career, ran for governor in large part to address the state's financial problems.[43]

It has been said that the only truly American contribution to philosophy is pragmatism.[44] It is not surprising, then, that this is the type of third party that wins elections in the United States. Pragmatism, in the sense of being realistic and practical, is one of the most exalted virtues in the American cultural landscape (indeed, Gillespie finds in his research that even many doctrinaire third parties are split between the purists and those willing to be a bit more practical about things). It is in this regard, then, that if a third party can avoid being constrained by an ideology or set of issues and instead embraces a wide-ranging pragmatic approach to government, it positions itself for electoral success.

These parties are also utilitarian. Not beholden to any platform—because the parties are pragmatic—the candidates can pick and choose their positions for their electoral advantage. King, Weicker, and Ventura, for example, are all socially liberal but also pro-business, and they to different degrees presented themselves as anti-waste government managers. Hickel was also very pro-business (a source of his victory being his opponents' environmentalism), and though he is socially conservative, this stance is utilitarian inasmuch as he was running in a state that was growing in its conservatism.[45]

These types of third-party candidates tend to straddle the relative ideological middle, enabling themselves to maximize their votes in a

Downsian sense, and so in some regard these parties are akin to the two major parties, who try to cast as wide a net as possible over the electorate, less concerned with ideology than with power.[46] But the utilitarian label is germane in a more important sense, in that they can loose themselves of party labels and the pigeonholing attached to them. They can define themselves as they choose, and then often vaguely—as independent, a reformer, above politics and partisanship—and let voters project onto them their own set of values, as voters have been shown to do when ignorant of a candidate's stances.[47] The key, then, is not so much that these candidates are moderate in the contemporary, popular sense, but rather that the pragmatist-utilitarian is able to become all things to all people. The most important thing is that they are independent, an alternative from outside the system. (Even Weicker, who had a long and noted career as a Republican with a clear record to study, is nearly impossible to define: an early proponent of the Americans with Disabilities Act, an advocate for AIDS research, an essential civil libertarian who opposed school prayer—all this and a onetime Republican.)

Of course, candidates benefit from a major party label by being associated with their party's issues. That association, however, is the pragmatist-utilitarian's advantage over his or her major party rivals. A candidate of a major party benefits from the party label when voters make their decisions about candidates based on *associations* with their party's issues. However, they are also associated with things a voter does *not* like about their party. And, as Stephen Ansolabehere and Shanto Iyengar demonstrate in *Going Negative,*

> Democrats, for instance, are considered proponents of social welfare and other public assistance programs, while Republicans are seen as protectors of business interests and supporters of a strong military. These stereotypes and expectations, however crude, enable voters to form beliefs about particular candidates' positions on issues.[48]

After an extensive series of experiments, Ansolabehere and Iyengar conclude that "voters give little credence to promises by candidates that do not fit with their partisan reputations."[49] In other words, candidates of major parties both benefit *and* suffer from a major party label. They cannot break out of its popularly conceived-of parameters, which is reinforced by the media's oversimplification of issues and tendency to present almost caricature-like pictures of politicians. They are unable to dissociate themselves from things voters do not like about the party, even if the candidates themselves have a different stance. This is precisely the opening available to the pragmatic-utilitarian.

A candidate from a pragmatist third party is loosed of these bonds. He can be what he will in voters' minds because his party, if he has one, is not known for anything. Thus, Angus King's status as an independent fits the pragmatic-utilitarian pattern. Of course, this imposes information costs on voters because they have to learn about the candidate to a greater degree than they consider necessary for the major party candidates—they already know what those parties are more or less about, anyway—and there is a danger that voters might conclude that educating themselves is not worth the time.

However, a pragmatist third-party candidate has several factors counteracting this potential problem. The first is modern political advertising. Part of the reason advertising is so important to a third-party bid, in addition to conferring legitimacy, is that it helps educate the electorate. Ansolabehere and Iyengar demonstrated in their studies that contrary to laments by some political commentators to the contrary, voters can be and are educated by a campaign's television advertising. The perfect example of how a third party can do this is Hillsman's "Thinker" ad during the Ventura campaign, which he created with the express intent of showing female voters the "softer" side of Ventura—husband, father, volunteer coach, a man interested in improving public education.[50] Thus, if a pragmatist-utilitarian third-party campaign can educate voters on the candidate and his or her issues—ease information costs, in other words—then that candidate can be freed of the confines of a major party label while not suffering the disadvantage of not having such a label.

The second factor working in favor of a pragmatist third-party candidate is the dramatic shift in American politics from party-centered races to almost completely candidate-centered races. Voters are less attached to a given party and more willing to vote for a specific candidate, and thus a politician's personality, experience, and own stands on different issues weigh for many voters far more than his or her belonging to a given party.[51] Thus a third-party candidate is more able in the modern political landscape to get a serious look from voters *as an individual running for office* (as discussed, these four governors had high name recognition before running and were therefore able to get more attention *as individuals*).[52] Indeed, many people have active antipathy toward what they see as the polarizing rigidity of the two major parties, and many people believe that the "with it" thing to be is an "independent."

The third factor that works in favor of utilitarian third-party candidates is the documented tendency of voters who like a candidate personally to project onto the individual their own values; that is, when voters like a candidate for one reason, they can often make the leap that they probably agree with the person in many other ways as well.[53] Since he or she lacks the major-party label that helps to pigeonhole candidates, it is reasonable to believe that projecting is more pronounced with prominent third-party candidates.[54] People can easily project their values on a candidate whom they find attractive personally or whose "independence" they appreciate but about whose issue priorities and positions they know little. If Governor Carlson is correct that "the name of the game is defining your opponent," then the difficulty of defining a third-party candidate is seen well in the example of Jesse Ventura. Professors Stephen Frank and Steven Wagner of St. Cloud State University seemed somewhat confounded as they tried to define what exactly he is:

> He is not a liberal. He does not support gun control nor government assisted child care. He is not a conservative. He supports abortion rights and the rights of gays. He is not really a centrist. A centrist would never articulate positions such as favoring . . . eliminating minimum wage laws. As a candidate he never stayed on issue and always deflected tough questions about policy positions to his competitors and the media. Nonetheless, he still obtained 773,713 votes.[55]

People want to define candidates because it makes voting for or against them simple. But if a candidate can avoid being defined, some voters will nonetheless conclude that they understand what this person is all about, which is most obviously that he or she is independent and above the wretchedness of "partisan politics." It is interesting to note, for example, that Ventura won the plurality of the self-identified liberal vote and that King's campaign was described as tending to lack specifics.[56] Many people knew that Hickel was conservative, for example, but his decision to run as an independent may have been seen by some as indicative of a shift in his ideology. So, too, with Weicker: Here was a person, widely regarded as a man of integrity, who, after serving the state and making a name as a Republican, left the GOP (or as he told it, the GOP left him) and formed a third party, to stand above politics, to be independent.

The drawbacks of lacking a party label to aid voters' decisions thus mitigated, it is easy to see that running as a pragmatist-utilitarian third party could be more advantageous than running in one of the major parties. If the candidate during the campaign can reach the state of "legitimacy," then the advantage shifts to the pragmatist-utilitarian. And each of the common aspects of these four candidacies—the availability of financing, the candidates' name recognition, the weakness of the other candidates—can all be rightly seen as variables that, in these specific cases, afforded them an easier road to legitimate status as a candidate.

One important aspect of pragmatist-utilitarian third-party success is that the examples here span different economic and social conditions. Whereas Lowell Weicker was elected during a recession and a state budget crisis, Walter Hickel, elected the same year, won when most voters in his state were happy with the state and optimistic about its future (paying no income taxes and receiving Alaska's Permanent Fund Dividend checks every year). Even so, Hickel won because a significant part of the electorate thought he "represented change and getting rid of politics as usual; they wanted to shake up state government, cut spending and get rid of yuppie bureaucrats."[57] King was elected as Maine's economy began to pick up after the recession,[58] and Ventura was elected in the most economically plush time in Minnesota's history. In other words, the utilitarian party appears to not require the impetus of some major problem, as the splinter-secessionist third parties do. Further, it is a type of third party capable of operating in parity with Democrats and Republicans. It may also be the case that its probability of success rises with the economic tide: Voters become more comfortable with taking a risk on someone who will alter the system and not just policy.

Again, it is important to keep in mind that the groundwork of this new theory of third parties relies on only four examples, which naturally limits the degree to which strong inferences can be made (it is an entirely different matter to study presidential politics, where the electoral college and the enormity of such an effort—access to all fifty states' ballots, for example—become nearly impossibly large barriers). Further analysis of the elections in Alaska, Connecticut, and Maine, in the fashion that I have investigated the Minnesota election, would be worthwhile. This groundwork, however, does serve to offer a direction in which the study of third parties might proceed.

Political Culture Reconsidered

Social scientists are disinclined to discuss cultural influences on political and economic outcomes. They hate it first because it is unpopular in academia to discuss such things, and they hate it doubly because they cannot quantify it. But such things, if they matter, will not go away. In fact, with works like Robert Putnam's *Bowling Alone* and its exploration of the decline of American civic engagement now gaining attention, perhaps the election of Jesse Ventura will aid its reconsideration.

Minnesota's historical tendency toward populism and general willingness to usurp the political order was discussed in this book's introduction. Though not offered as a cultural explanation in itself, this political culture helped birth the electoral system that allowed Ventura to
get elected. So which came first, the chicken or the egg? The culture or
the system? And what can we say about the simple lack of attachment
to a two-party order? Or a willingness to innovate (that even *The Economist* lauded in its discussions of the state)?

In this vein, it is perhaps not surprising that the other states exam-
ined here—Maine, Alaska, and Connecticut—display some of the same
tendencies. Mainers are famously stubborn and independent; in fact,
prior to the current spat of third-party governors in the 1990s, Maine
was the sole state to elect a governor from a third party since 1942.
Alaska, likewise, has its own bizarre political self, mostly related to an
ambivalent relationship with the federal government and the lower
states generally. And it is probably not a coincidence that by some estimates Connecticut has the highest number of independent voters in the
nation.[59]

This is all tepid evidence, to be sure. But it does suggest that, at the
very least, political science's collective hesitance to dive into the murky
waters of the meaning of political culture is misguided, if not somehow
intellectually dishonest.

Notes

1. Tom Wolfe, *The Kandy-Kolored Tangerine-Flake Streamline Baby* (New
York: Noonday Press, 1963), p. 6 of the introduction.
2. David T. Canon, professor of political science, University of Wisconsin,
8 March 2000, *Jesse* (e-mail note to the author).
3. Randy Skoglund, Republican Party official and Coleman campaign
worker, 18 August 1999, telephone interview by the author, Mahtomedi, MN, to
Minneapolis, MN.
4. Jesse Ventura, *I Ain't Got Time to Bleed* (New York: Villard, 1999), p. 87.
5. The others being Idaho, Wyoming, New Hampshire, Wisconsin, and
New Hampshire; North Dakota has no registration. See the Federal Election
Commission's "Frequently Asked Questions About Voter Registration and Voting," available on the Internet at http://www.fec.gov/pages/faqs.htm.
6. State of Minnesota, Secretary of State's Office, *Minnesota Election Statistics 1950–1998* (St. Paul: Secretary of State's Office). Available on the Internet at http://www.sos.state.mn.us.
7. 15.79 percent of the voters were same-day registrants, which means, according to the ecologically determined point value of those voting for Ventura

(69.6 percent), that 10.98 percent of the total turnout were same-day registrants voting for Ventura.

8. Steven Rosenstone and Raymand Wolfinger, *Who Votes?* (New Haven: Yale University Press, 1980), p. 17.

9. Rosenstone and Wolfinger, *Who Votes?* p. 18.

10. Ibid.

11. Ben Highton, "Easy Registration and Voter Turnout," *Journal of Politics* 59 (May 1997), pp. 565–575.

12. State of Minnesota, Secretary of State's Office, *Minnesota Election Statistics 1950–1998*.

13. The rise in turnout among low-educated voters might be even greater for two reasons. First, for purposes here, people who had had "some college" were left out of the calculations; however, this group could contain people who attended some form of trade school. Exit polls are a suspect source of data; see Andrea L. Campbell and Bradley Palmquist, "Exit Polls as a Source of Political Data," *1998 Annual Meeting of the American Political Science Association* (Boston: APSA, 1998).

14. Mary McEvoy, former associate chair of the DFL and Freeman campaign outreach director, 22 July 1999, telephone interview by the author, Cambridge, MA, to Minneapolis, MN.

15. Recalled by Phil Madsen during an interview with the author, 2 September 1999.

16. Those with lower incomes ($30,000 or less) were a greater share of the electorate in 1990 and 1994, and so any investigation of income as related to voting is pointless. This decline is probably related to the fact that Minnesotans' personal incomes have increased on average almost 40 percent since 1990, at which point there was a recession. Moreover, Rosenstone and Wolfinger found income to be a far less important variable for turnout than education.

17. KSTP-TV, St. Paul, "Young Voters." Aired 3 November 1998. Videocassette of newscast given to author by KSTP-TV.

18. Ruy Teixeira, *Why Americans Don't Vote: Turnout Decline in the United States 1960–1984* (Westport: Greenwood Press, 1987), pp. 28–29.

19. Steven J. Rosenstone, Roy L. Behr, and Edward H. Lazarus, *Third Parties in America* (Princeton: Princeton University Press, 1996), pp. 107–110.

20. Phil Madsen interview, 2 September 1999.

21. This might be oversimplified; the disparate polling might have to do with other factors, such as the attention people gave him during the state fair versus the debates, or with the content of what he was saying, or the level and quality of media coverage during each period.

22. Arne Carlson, outgoing Republican governor of Minnesota, 9 September 1999, interview by the author, Minneapolis, MN.

23. Rosenstone, Behr, and Lazarus, *Third Parties in America,* p. 1.

24. Alan Shilepsky, former Reform Party candidate for Minnesota Secretary of State, 15 August 1999, telephone interview by the author, Mahtomedi, MN, to Minneapolis, MN.

25. Rosenstone, Behr, and Lazarus, *Third Parties in America,* p. 121.

26. Ibid., pp. 107–110.

27. J. David Gillespie, *Politics at the Periphery* (Columbia: University of South Carolina Press, 1993), pp. 9–10.

28. It of course depends on whom one asks; the individual members of these parties may not prefer to see themselves this way.

29. Gillespie, *Politics at the Periphery*, p. 10.

30. In *The Discourses,* Niccolo Machiavelli contradicts arguments that Rome was undone by extending freedom of speech to the plebeians, asserting instead that the Roman Republic's stability was precisely due to this liberality, as it allowed plebian discontent to be vented and diffused; he writes, "To which I answer that every city should provide ways and means whereby the ambitions of the populace may find an outlet." See Niccolo Machiavelli, *The Discourses,* trans. Leslie Walker, ed. Bernard Crick (London: Penguin Books, 1950), Book I, Discourse 4.

31. Gillespie, *Politics at the Periphery*, pp. 302–305.

32. Thomas J. Collins, "Humphrey, Coleman Wary of 'Everyman' Ventura," *St. Paul Pioneer Press*, 24 September 1998, p. 1A.

33. Michael Barone and Grant Ujifusa, *The Almanac of American Politics 1992* (Washington: National Journal Inc., 1991), pp. 212–214.

34. Hickel also waited until less than an hour before the deadline to file for governor, something some observers say prevented his opponents from getting a chance to attack him.

35. Ibid., p. 29.

36. Rob Mintz, assistant attorney general of Alaska, 9 March 2000, *Hickel* (e-mail note to the author).

37. Reverend Linwood Arnold, longtime resident of Maine, 11 March 2000, telephone conversation with the author, Cambridge, MA, to South Portland, ME.

38. Michael Barone and Grant Ujifusa, *The Almanac of American Politics 1996* (Washington: National Journal Inc., 1995,), p. 590.

39. A. Jay Higgins, "Snowe, Baldacci Claim Victory; King-Brennan Race a Toss-up," *Bangor Daily News*, 9 November 1994, p. 1A.

40. Barone and Ujifusa, *The Almanac of American Politics 1996,* p. 593.

41. John F. Bibby and L. Sandy Maisel, *Two Parties—Or More?* (Boulder: Westview Press, 1998), p. 81.

42. See the LUC Media website at http://www.lucmedia.com/mkst.html.

43. And of course a very convincing argument can be made that achievements such as obtaining a balanced budget or getting a cumbersome bureaucracy or tax system out of people's way are noble in their own right; they're just less interesting than declaring war on poverty or something like that.

44. Pragmatism emerged in American thought toward the end of the nineteenth century, originally formulated by Charles S. Pierce and gaining wide appreciation through William James and John Dewey. At the base of what is in fact a complex and wide-ranging school of philosophy is the connection between thought and action, but the idea that pragmatism extols the commonsense person who has a distaste for theoretical thought and favors "actions over words" is, in fact, not the case. This idea of the "practical man" is, however, the one that has become popularized and in many regards is the form taken in American life, and it is thus the one most relevant to our politics. Gillespie discusses this in *Politics at the Periphery.*

45. Rob Mintz, 9 March 2000, *Hickel* (e-mail note to the author).

46. Gillespie, in comparing them to minor parties, finds that the major parties are fundamentally nonideological and malleable in what they stand for; those who complain that the major parties stand for nothing are in this view correct.

47. See Gregory B. Markus and Phillip E. Converse, "A Dynamic Simultaneous Equation Model of Electoral Choice," in Richard G. Niemi and Herbert Weisberg, eds., *Classics in Voting Behavior* (Washington: Congressional Quarterly Inc., 1993), pp. 146–149.

48. Stephen Ansolabehere and Shanto Iyengar, *Going Negative: How Political Advertisements Shrink and Polarize the Electorate* (New York: Free Press, 1995), p. 42.

49. Ibid., p. 85.

50. Bill Hillsman, CEO of North Woods Advertising and Ventura campaign media consultant, 26 August 1999, interview by the author, Minneapolis, MN.

51. John Aldrich finds this to be unambiguously the case, writing in *Why Parties?* "Here the evidence is clear. The proportions and strength of party attachments in the electorate declined in the mid-1960s. . . . The behavioral consequences are if anything even clearer. Defection from party lines and split-ticket voting are more common for all major offices. . . . Elections are more candidate centered and less party centered, and those who come to office have played a greater role in shaping their own more highly personalized electoral coalitions." See James Aldrich, *Why Parties? The Origin and Transformation of Political Parties in America* (Chicago: University of Chicago Press, 1995), p. 17.

52. When asked whether he thought people were voting for him or for the Reform Party in general, Ventura replied, "Probably me. Because if you look at it they voted for me and then went back and voted for the two other parties for the other offices." (Governor Jesse Ventura, 6 October 1999, discussion with the author, Cambridge, MA.)

53. See Markus and Converse, "A Dynamic Simultaneous Equation Model of Electoral Choice," pp. 146–149.

54. Reading the internal Republican tracking poll verbal responses, I was surprised to find people intending to vote for Ventura who thought he held a position on some issue that he in fact did not.

55. Stephen I. Frank and Steven C. Wagner, *"We Shocked the World!" A Case Study of Jesse Ventura's Election as Governor of Minnesota* (Fort Worth: Harcourt College Publishers, 1999), p. 29.

56. See Barone and Ujifusa, *The Almanac of American Politics 1996*, p. 590.

57. Charles Wohlforth, "Hickel's Victory Came on 'Wild Card' Vote," *Anchorage Daily News*, 25 November 1990, p. A1.

58. Jay Higgens, "Snowe, Baldacci Claim Victory, " p. 1A; he writes of "Maine's finances and revenue projections charting a modest recovery after plummeting in the 1990 recession."

59. Senator Chris Dodd (D-CT), 15 February 2000, presentation at the Kennedy School of Government, Harvard University, Cambridge, MA.

5

CONCLUSION

The concomitant question usually asked along with how and why Jesse Ventura became Governor Ventura—the basic question of this book—is whether we should properly view his election as a good thing or a bad thing. Debating the merits and demerits of his holding office is probably a lot more interesting than reading about the minutia of policy or the academic value of his election, and it has become a sort of pastime among people who otherwise would not spend a great deal of time thinking about what it means to be alive in a democratic political society.

Opinions are diverse. For some, this election and this man are a rebirth of freedom, the triumph of democracy over everything wrong with America. There are those who view Ventura as the only honest politician in America, and also there are those who think of him as someone in a strong position to radically alter the American political landscape in ways that restore people's confidence in government. Some just like his worldview—government out of your way, fend for yourself—and still others like that he allows numerous caveats to his libertarianism. There is, in other words, something here for everyone; he has indeed become all things to all people.

The triumph of American anti-intellectualism is how a number of other people see it. According to this line of reasoning, Ventura is the perfection of our ability to be impressed by shallowness. That a man with no experience of any real sort, a relatively shallow understanding of government, and a potpourri of empty slogans was elected in a state whose people are regarded for picking statesmen only demonstrates how completely America has declined. The fall is not far behind, as self-restraint, the most important virtue in a democracy, breaks down to a point of throwing one's vote away on entertainment in the form of a politician. The anti-intellectual populism he used in the campaign, attacking people with college degrees, for instance, and making a big deal about being the only candidate who didn't have a law degree (apparently ignorant of James Madison's belief that this was the exactly right class to legislate), frightens many people, and his minimalist view of government combined with his rabid self-promotion leads many to ask the question, how little can we possibly expect of ourselves and our leaders?

People can try to adjudicate the pros and cons of Governor Ventura all they want—and they do—but at the end of the day it doesn't really matter, because the question itself is mostly irrelevant. There is an extent to which what happens in a nation's political life cannot be said to be good or bad. It simply is. In a democracy, the primary arbiter of good and bad is the will of the people; in this instance the people have spoken, they have cast their votes (and more of them than usual, too), giving Ventura's victory a certain procedural justice, and they did it in the open, freely, without tanks or troops guarding the capital. The most central goal of a democracy is its own preservation and stability (thus, in times of war everything changes, and personal liberty can be made to take a backseat to national security, permitted by the courts, who reflect an understanding of the import of stability more generally in their being loath to reverse and contradict earlier rulings). In a democratic society, stability is dependent on the people's belief in the legitimacy of their institutions. And if a greater share of them feel engaged in their government because of Ventura, if more of them vote and more of them trust their leaders, then that is a good in and of itself. There is, in other words, a justice in stability.

At the same time, if Jesse Ventura achieves and maintains his mandate by convincing people that their government is broken, that all politicians save him are dishonest, that the system is itself so corrupt that it no longer is worth dealing in as it exists, then things are less stable, and that is in the same way bad.

As for Ventura himself, only time will tell what impact he will have in American politics. He has now left the Reform Party, because he did not want to share it with Pat Buchanan (interestingly, though Ventura himself is the embodiment of pragmatism, he assumed the mantle of the purist when he chose to leave the party rather than grow its base with Buchanan's people; in a major party there would be room for everyone, more or less). He is now the de facto head of the Independence Party in Minnesota. His party was completely shut out of the 2000 elections, even after a major effort to recruit and run candidates for as many seats as possible; this is ultimately unsurprising, and, whatever Ventura's own future, his party is in poor shape.

As governor, he has, as of this writing, signed a sales tax rebate, and he initiated the beginnings of a light rail system meant to deal with the traffic in the state. For a while he pushed for a unicameral legislature, believing that it is between the House and the Senate that politicians make deals with lobbyists, but he now seems to have given up on it for lack of public interest.

What has probably received the lion's share of the attention, though, has been his private adventuring. Always restrained in his understatement and never crippled by self-awareness, Governor Ventura has said he considers his elected office a part-time job, meaning, in his mind, that he has plenty of time for other things as well, including writing two books, refereeing a professional wrestling match (for which he earned over a million dollars and during which he swore on television), and becoming an announcer for the XFL. He is very, very certain that profiting from an elected office, at least in his case and the way he does it, is not a problem, is not something that could ultimately hurt the perceived legitimacy of the office itself. He pleads, when pressed, that he has only to answer to the people of Minnesota. Of course, he's right inasmuch as the proper existence of a democracy does rely on the goodness of the people, who govern themselves and hold their right to judge their leaders, but it also depends on the goodness of those leaders to control and police themselves, for a person in a position of public trust can easily do a great deal of harm unseen. It is not unfair or unreasonable to assert that elected office as a source of profit, even if a plurality of people say that they are fine with it, is not a function that will in the long term improve people's regard for government or the culture of how government functions. Ventura has even suggested that his wife should get a salary for putting up with the burden of being the First Lady of Minnesota. These actions have made many people angry, but Ventura has been allowed to get away with things that no other Minnesota politician ever could, like saying that religion was for the weak-minded. History will judge the value of Ventura's time in office, but for the time being, he has by his own choices marked his tenure, whatever his legislative accomplishments or impressive grasp of many issues.

As for the other participants in the election, Skip Humphrey and Mike Freeman took jobs in the private sector. Ted Mondale's moderation earned him a job offer from Ventura as the head of the Metropolitan Council, charged with overseeing much of the infrastructure (the bus system, sewage, housing development) in the seven counties around the Twin Cities, which he took. Norm Coleman is still mayor of St. Paul, and recently he announced that he will run for the Senate seat against Paul Wellstone in 2002. Mark Dayton finally got what he had always wanted by purchasing himself a U.S. Senate seat in 2000.

The basic purpose of this book was to examine the source of Jesse Ventura's victory in the 1998 Minnesota gubernatorial election, to answer the question of why he was able to win as a third-party candidate when most others get nowhere. I hope I did this in an analytical manner and with an absence of value judgments. If I did, that may be the book's distinguishing feature and its greatest merit.

As for the specific arguments of this book, some of them can more or less stand on their own—the study of what drives the individual decision to vote, or the layering of lessons for studying celebrity politics and the importance of electoral rules to Ventura's victory and to political outcomes in general; all these will probably meet with little resistance.

Others among them are more speculative and may not be accepted as quickly; for instance, the argument in favor of the belief that politics are shaped by perceptions, and how much perceptions shape what people perceive as real, in effect creating a reality unto itself (in this case, for third parties). Or the discussion on the way the media can influence political outcome through the perceptions of reality they deliver to their audience. (There are innumerable schools of thought on how the media may or may not affect politics, people's beliefs, how people think of themselves, and the like, but it is an interesting thought experiment to consider how the life of the country might be different if everyone read, say, *The Economist* instead of the *New York Times*.) These arguments are more speculative. Likewise, my argument that there is a type of third party capable of winning elections—one that in certain circumstances has an advantage over the major parties—is likely to meet with some wringing of hands and semantic dissection among people who care about such things.

They are likely to point out that such an event has not occurred at the national level, or that third-party candidate A or B failed in state Y or Z, or that this idea is based on a small number of cases. That is all fine. The distance of time will probably give a clearer picture of the value of the ideas in this book. In time, probably, more people will win office as candidates of third parties, and the story of those elections will support or deny the arguments made in this book. Perhaps some of these will be celebrities of Ventura's kind, and the hypotheses offered here on how celebrity politics functions in America will likewise be proven or denied. But until this happens, we are left to rely on our experiences with a man named Jesse.

APPENDIX A

UNOFFICIAL VOTE FOR GOVERNOR, BY COUNTY

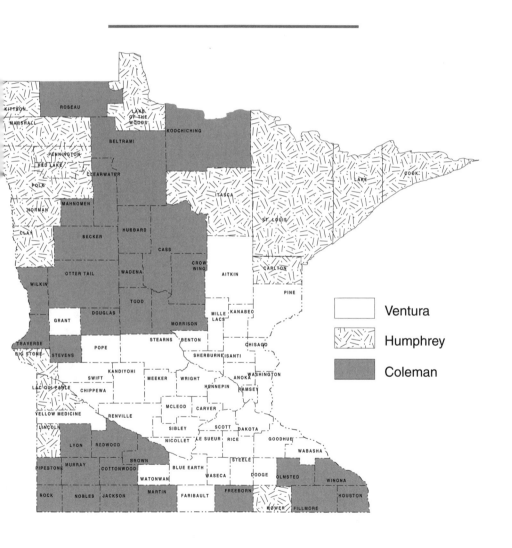

Ventura

Humphrey

Coleman

135

APPENDIX B

POLL RESULTS DURING THE RACE FOR GOVERNOR

Detail of the Polls

	Ventura	Humphrey	Coleman	Undecided
May 29–June 1 (MN Poll)	10	44	34	12
May 30–June 1 *(Pioneer Press)*	7	46	30	17
July 25–30 (MN GOP)	16	40	35	9
July 23–28 *(Star Tribune)*	11	39	35	15
August 28–30 *(Pioneer Press)*	13	43	29	15
September 3–8 (MN GOP)	14	38	38	10
September 8–11 *(Star Tribune)*	13	41	31	15
September 16–20 *(Star Tribune)*	10	49	29	12
September 26–28 (MN GOP)	15	42	32	11
October 7–8 (Sen. Rod Grams) (Tarrance)	21	34	37	8
October 10–13 *(Pioneer Press)*	15	44	31	10
October 11–13 (MN GOP)	21	34	32	13
October 13–15 (MN GOP)	22	36	32	10
October 15–18 *(Star Tribune)*	21	35	34	10
October 18–22 (MN GOP)	24	33	33	10
October 23–25 *(Pioneer Press)*	23	34	33	10
October 24–26 (MN GOP)	27	29	33	11
October 25–27 (MN GOP)	27	29	32	12

Figure B.1 Polls Over Time

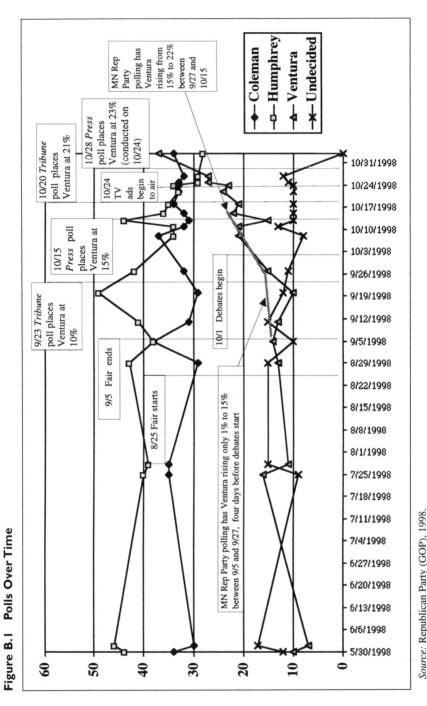

Source: Republican Party (GOP), 1998.

Note: The polling discounted people who were not registered even if they claimed that they intended to vote: The last entry in the poll thus represents a smaller movement (especially for Ventura) than it appears, since many of the people who voted for him and had intended to do so throughout were not

CONTENT ANALYSIS

Explanation of Content Analysis Scoring

The content analysis for this project was performed by sampling fifty-five articles, twenty-five from the Minneapolis *Star Tribune* and thirty from the *St. Paul Pioneer Press*. These were selected by a random sample of every fourth article from the period of 27 August 1998 to 3 November 1998. There were at times, for example, three articles, one about each of the candidates, run on the same day, and it seemed prudent to break the random pattern and sample all three for the sake of comparison. Also, at times a chosen article would be an insignificant blurb or an editorial, and these were left out. The same four-pronged content analysis was performed on all articles according to the following rules.

Ventura Legitimacy Analysis

Legitimacy Points were assigned only for Jesse Ventura. This scoring was meant to quantify the perception by the media and their presentation of Ventura's legitimacy as a candidate (assuming that Humphrey and Coleman were legitimate from the start, they were excluded here). A negative legitimacy point was awarded any time an article referenced the Ventura campaign as a side event or cast doubt on its legitimacy; this includes references to him as a "long shot," a spoiler for the other two, an oddball, or a comical candidate with little chance of winning. Two negative legitimacy points were given for any headline featuring both Humphrey and Coleman where Ventura might have reasonably been included along with the other two, but was not; an example of this would be an article comparing positions on education that has the other two candidates in the headline minus Ventura. There was also a negative legitimacy point given for articles such as those just described if they discussed all candidates on a particular issue but mentioned Ventura only at the very end of the article, in less than two paragraphs. Additionally, a negative legitimacy point was given when there were simultaneous "candidate profiles" on Coleman and Humphrey but not Ventura. Positive legitimacy points were given for any treatment of him as being a "real" candidate; this includes references to him as "credible" or as a "contender," and suggestions that he might win or at least beat one of the other two. Two positive legitimacy points were given for inclusion in a headline along with the other two candidates, and one legitimacy point was given for any time an article about candidates on a specific issue turned its gaze to Ventura before one or both of the other two candidates. One positive legitimacy point was given when "candidate profiles" were done on the candidates and included Ventura.

Media Scrutiny Analysis

Scrutiny Points were assigned each time (one point per instance) an article questioned or cast doubt on a candidate's person, proposals, ability, or record.

Personal Qualities Presentation Analysis

Personal Points were assigned on both a positive and a negative scale. Positive personal points were assigned each time an article made mention of a positive aspect of a candidate's personality, be it honesty, the common touch, work ethic, intelligence, sense of humor, friendliness, or an aspect of his personal history (such as having served in the military). Negative personal points were given any time an article made mention of something that could be seen as a negative personality trait, such as (most commonly) dishonesty, duplicity, elitism, a bad temper, lack of intelligence, or a negative side to the candidate's personal history. No distinction was made between instances of a quote within an article as said by someone (offering his or her inherently biased opinion) and an instance within the regular text of the article, according to the line of reasoning that regardless of whether the article or a third party quoted within the article is saying something positive or negative about a candidate, it is still being related to the reader's mind. One point (positive or negative) was assigned for each instance, ignoring severity of the comment, and a score was given for both positive personal points and negative personal points (that is, they were not added for a net effect).

Governing Ability Presentation Analysis

Governing Points were assigned in a similar fashion as personal points, but for *how* a candidate would perform as governor. In contrast to the relative ease with which mentions of personal qualities can be assessed, the proper assignment of governing points is slightly more ineffable, because, quite simply, one person's positive hypothetical decision as governor is another person's negative. Some aspects of governing—leadership ability, for example—are unambiguously good; others, such as a greater role for government in people's lives, are not, and these were excluded from this analysis. This created a dilemma that made this section more tentative than the others. For purposes here, any ambiguous trait of governing (e.g., wanting to expand the role of government) was left out of the analysis in favor of objectively good or bad traits (e.g., leadership).

Figure C.1 represents the press's portrayal of Ventura's "legitimacy" as a candidate, using a scoring system of positive and negative legitimacy points. Figure C.2 represents the media portrayal of the positive and negative personal aspects (e.g., "honesty" or "dishonesty") of each candidate. Figure C.3 represents the portrayal of each candidate's governing ability in positive and negative terms. Figure C.4 illustrates the level of scrutiny directed at each of the three candidates during the race.

Figure C.1 Depiction of Ventura's Legitimacy (Content Analysis) Over Time

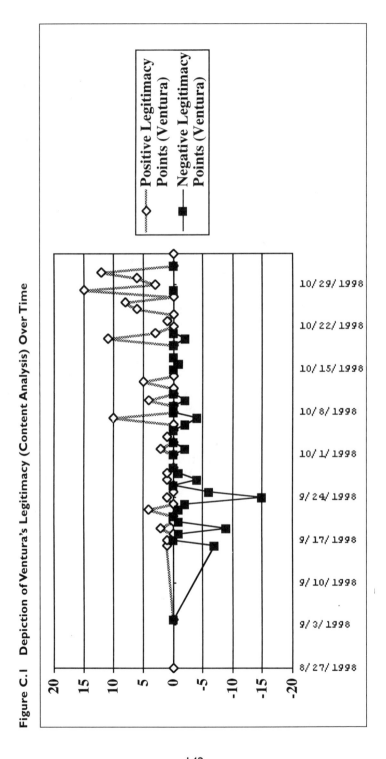

Figure C.2 Depiction of Personal Qualities (Content Analysis) Over Time

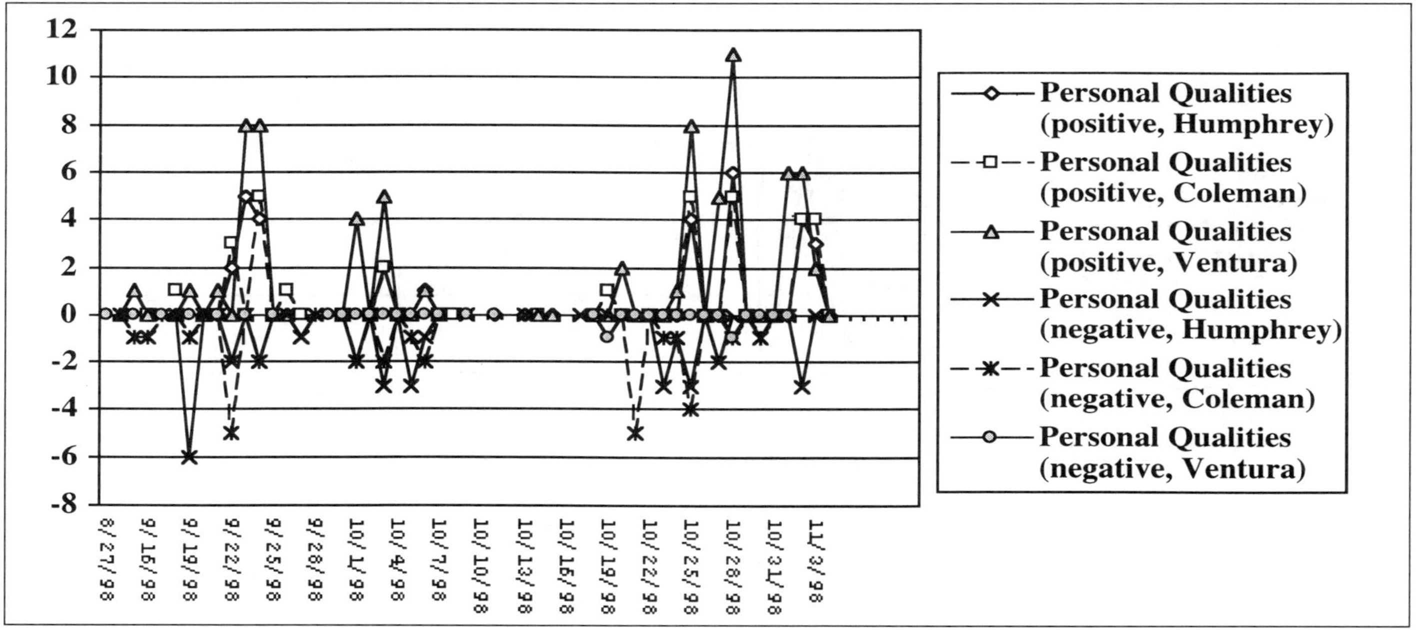

143

Figure C.3 Depiction of Governing Ability (Content Analysis) Over Time

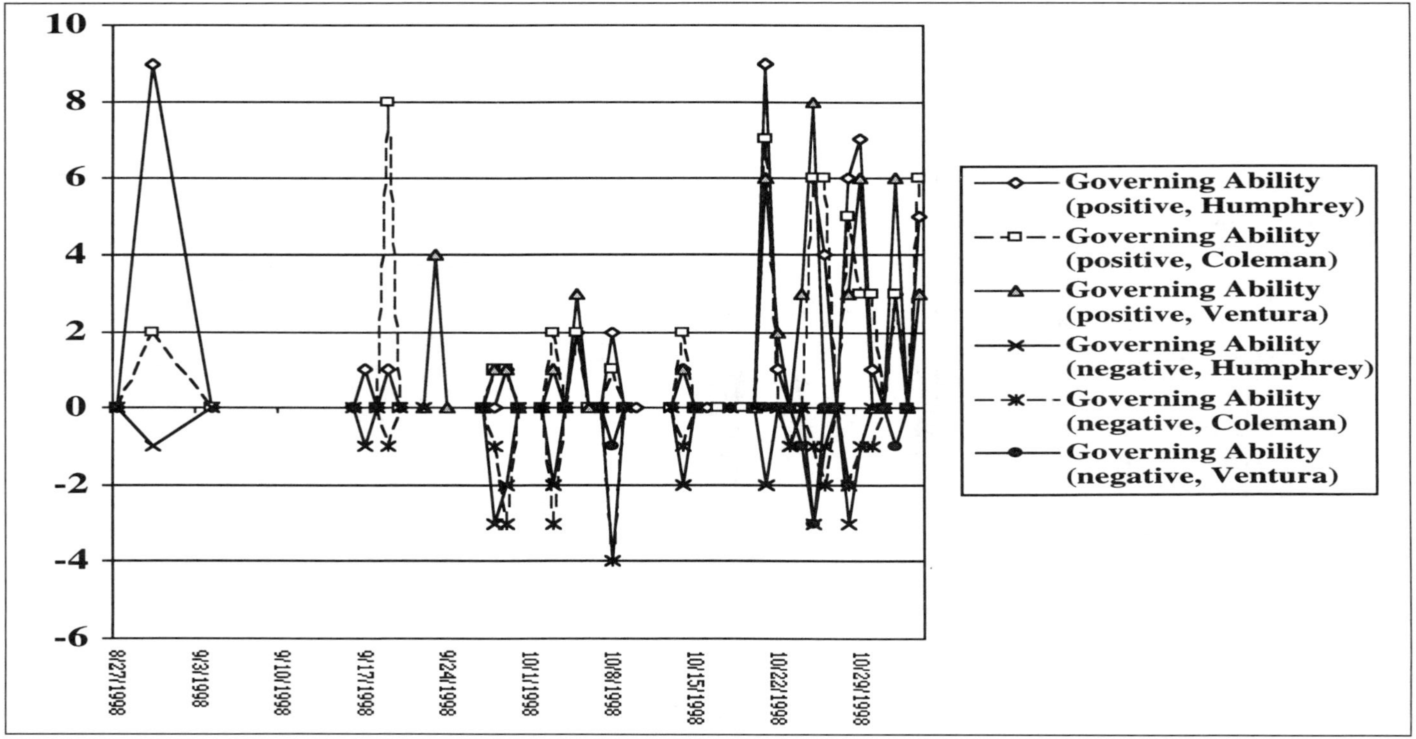

144

Figure C.4 Levels of Scrutiny (Content Analysis) Over Time

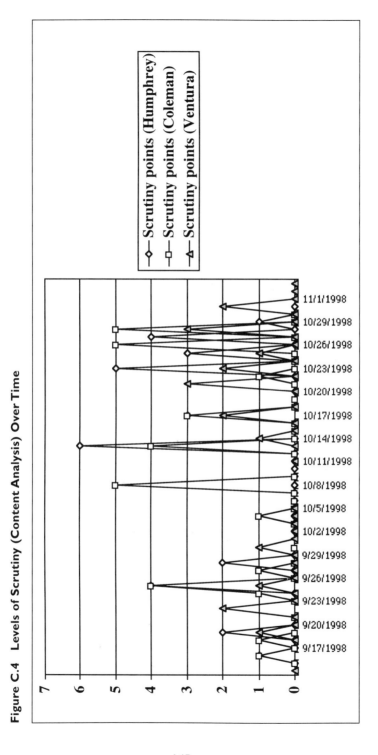

BIBLIOGRAPHY

Books

Aldrich, John H. 1995. *Why Parties? The Origin and Transformation of Political Parties in America.* Chicago: University of Chicago Press.

Ansolabehere, Stephen, and Shanto Iyengar. 1995. *Going Negative: How Political Advertisements Shrink and Polarize the Electorate.* New York: The Free Press.

Barone, Michael, and Grant Ujifusa. 1991. *The Almanac of American Politics 1992.* Washington: National Journal Inc.

———. 1993. *The Almanac of American Politics 1994.* Washington: National Journal Inc.

———. 1995. *The Almanac of American Politics 1996.* Washington: National Journal Inc.

———. 1998. *Two Parties—Or More?* Boulder, CO: Westview Press.

Califano, Joseph. 1991. *Triumph and Tragedy of Lyndon Johnson.* New York: Simon and Schuster.

Cohen, David T. 1990. *Actors, Athletes, and Astronauts: Political Amateurs in the United States Congress.* Chicago: University of Chicago Press.

Elazar, Daniel J. *American Federalism: A View from the States.* 1966. New York: Thomas Y. Crowell Company.

———, Virginia Gray, and Wyman Spano. 1999. *Minnesota Politics and Government.* Lincoln: University of Nebraska Press.

Eldersveld, Samuel J., and Hanes Walton Jr. 2000. *Political Parties in American Society.* 2nd ed. Boston: Bedford/St. Martin's Press.

Frank, Stephen I., and Steven C. Wagner. 1999. *"We Shocked the World!" A Case Study of Jesse Ventura's Election as Governor of Minnesota.* Fort Worth: Harcourt College Publishers.

Garrison, Webb. 1998. *A Treasury of Minnesota Tales.* Nashville: Rutledge Hill Press.

Gillespie, J. David. 1993. *Politics at the Periphery.* Columbia: University of South Carolina Press.

Jamieson, Kathleen Hall. 1992. *Dirty Politics: Deception, Distraction, and Democracy*. New York: Oxford University Press.
Krippendorff, Klaus. 1980. *Content Analysis: An Introduction to Its Methodology*. Newbury Park, CA: Sage Publications.
Lass, William E. 1998. *Minnesota: A History*. New York: W. W. Norton and Company.
Machiavelli, Niccolo. [1950] *The Discourses*. Book I, Discourse 4. Trans. Leslie J. Walker. Ed. Bernard Crick. London: Penguin Books.
Niemi, Richard G., and Herbert Weisberg, eds. 1993. *Classics in Voting Behavior*. Washington: Congressional Quarterly Inc.
Orren, Gary R., and Nelson W. Polsby. 1987. *Media and Momentum: The New Hampshire Primary and Nomination Politics*. Chatham, NJ: Chatham House Publishers.
Rosenstone, Steven J., Roy L. Behr, and Edward H. Lazarus. 1996. *Third Parties in America*. 2nd ed. Princeton: Princeton University Press.
————, and Raymond E. Wolfinger. 1980. *Who Votes?* New Haven: Yale University Press.
Teixeira, Ruy A. 1987. *Why Americans Don't Vote: Turnout Decline in the United States 1960–1984*. Westport, CT: Greenwood Press.
Ventura, Jesse. 1999. *I Ain't Got Time to Bleed: Reworking the Body Politic from the Bottom Up*. New York: Villard Books.
West, Cornel. 1989. *The American Evasion of Philosophy: A Genealogy of Pragmatism*. Madison: University of Wisconsin Press.
Wolfe, Tom. 1963. *The Kandy-Kolored Tangerine-Flake Streamline Baby*. New York: Noonday Press.

Magazine Articles

Highton, Ben. 1997. "Easy Registration and Voter Turnout." *Journal of Politics* 59 (May), pp. 565–575.
"Honesty Ranks First in Choosing Candidates." 30 November 1999. CNN.com, available at http://www.cnn.com/ALLPOLITICS/stories/1999/11/30/poll.ap/.
Keating, Holland. 12 October 1999. "Poll: Celebrity Presidential Candidates not Taken Seriously." CNN.com, available at http://www.cnn.com/ALLPOLITICS/stories/1999/10/12/poll.celebrities/.
"The Land of Good Lessons." 5 July 1997. *The Economist* 344 (8024), p. 28.
"Minnesota: A State That Works." 13 August 1973. *Time* 103 (7), p. 24.
Schier, Steven. January 1999. "Jesse's Victory: It Was No Fluke." *Washington Monthly* 31 (1). Available on the Internet at http://www.washingtonmonthly.com/features/1999/9901.schier.ventura.html.

Papers

Campbell, Andrea L., and Bradley Palmquist. "Exit Polls as a Source of Political Data." August 1998. *1998 Annual Meeting of the American Political Science Association*. Boston: APSA.

Personal Conversations

Arnold, Reverend Linwood. 11 March 2000. Telephone conversation with the author, Cambridge, MA, to South Portland, ME.

Bielick, Charlie. Director of Budget Planning, Minnesota Department of Finance. 9 March 2000. Telephone conversation with the author, Cambridge, MA, to St. Paul, MN.

Dodd, Senator Chris (D-CT). 15 February 2000. Conversation with the author. Cambridge, MA.

Gillaspy, Tom. Minnesota State Demographer. 21 June 2000. Telephone conversation with the author, Cambridge, MA, to St. Paul, MN.

Gritz, John P., Col.-SF (USA-Ret.). 16 August 1999. Telephone conversation with the author, Mahtomedi, MN, to Eagan, MN.

Olson, Jeanne. Executive Director of the Minnesota Campaign Finance and Public Disclosure Board. 24 February 1999. Telephone conversation with the author, Cambridge, MA, to St. Paul, MN.

Sawyer, Sally. Executive Director of the Minnesota League of Women Voters of Minnesota. 25 February 2000. Telephone conversation with the author, Cambridge, MA, to St. Paul, MN.

———. 28 August 2000. Telephone conversation with the author, Mahtomedi, MN, to St. Paul, MN.

Wolfe, Tom. 19 November 1999. Conversation with the author, Cambridge, MA.

Personal Correspondence

Canon, David T. Professor of Political Science, University of Wisconsin. 8 March 2000. *Jesse* (Internet, e-mail note to the author). Available from the author.

Czar, Kathy. Former DFL Party Executive Director. 19 February 2000. *Re:* (Internet, e-mail note to the author). Available from the author.

———. 5 March 2000. *Re:* (Internet, e-mail note to the author). Available from the author.

Fiorina, Morris. 21 February 2000. *Re:* (Internet, e-mail note to the author). Available from the author.

Madsen, Phil. 29 January 2000. *Re: Quick Questions* (Internet, e-mail note to the author). Available from the author.

———. 21 February 2000. *Re: Quick Questions* (Internet, e-mail note to the author). Available from the author.

———. 23 February 2000. *Re: Quick Questions* (Internet, e-mail note to the author). Available from the author.

———. 25 February 2000. *Re: Quick Questions* (Internet, e-mail note to the author). Available from the author.

Mintz, Rob. Assistant Attorney General of Alaska. 9 March 2000. *Hickel* (Internet, e-mail note to the author). Available from the author.

Rieve, Bob. 8 June 1999. Executive Director of SEAL of APPROVAL. *Re: Fw: Know a Good SEAL?* (Internet, e-mail note to John Gritz). Available from the author.

Telschow, Diana L. State Demographic Center. 15 February 2000. *Re: Data Posted to Form 1* (Internet, e-mail note to the author). Available from the author.
Verba, Sidney. 21 February 2000. *Re:* (Internet, e-mail note to the author). Available from the author.

Unpublished Interviews

Anderson, Terry. Reform Party activist/Ventura campaign worker. 14 August 2000. Telephone interview by the author in the Twin Cities.
Babcock, Bill. Director of the Silha Center for the Study of Media Ethics and Law at the University of Minnesota. 16 August 1999. Telephone interview by the author, Mahtomedi, MN, to Minneapolis, MN.
Barkley, Dean. Chairman of the Minnesota Planning Commission and Ventura campaign manager. 3 August 1999. Interview by the author, St. Paul, MN.
Carlson, Arne. Outgoing Republican governor. 9 September 1999. Interview by the author, Minneapolis, MN.
Carlson, Tony. DFL activist and Ventura campaign volunteer. 20 July 1999. Telephone interview by the author, Cambridge, MA, to Minneapolis, MN.
Cooper, Bill. Chair of the Minnesota Republican Party. 3 September 1999. Interview by the author, Wayzata, MN.
Czar, Kathy. Former DFL Executive Director. 21 July 1999. Telephone interview by the author, Cambridge, MA, to Minneapolis, MN.
Dietz, Dick. Vice-chair of the Minnesota Reform Party. 28 July 1999. Telephone interview by the author, Cambridge, MA, to Mankota, MN.
Escala, Eric. WCCO (CBS affiliate) political reporter. 26 July 1999. Telephone interview by the author, Cambridge, MA, to Minneapolis, MN.
Evans, Denn. Alan Shilepsky's Secretary of State campaign chair. 20 August 1999. Telephone interview by the author, Mahtomedi, MN, to St. Cloud, MN.
Franchett, Gene. Ventura campaign worker. 28 July 1999. Telephone interview by the author, Cambridge, MA, to Minneapolis, MN.
Freeman, Mike. Endorsed DFL candidate for governor. 27 August 1999. Interview by the author, Minneapolis, MN.
Fridley, Russell. Former Director of the Minnesota Historical Society. 2 August 1999. Telephone interview by the author, Mahtomedi, MN, to St. Paul, MN.
Friedline, Doug. Ventura campaign manager. 1 September 1999. Interview by the author, St. Paul, MN.
Georgacas, Chris. Former Chairman of the Republican Party of Minnesota and Coleman campaign manager. 4 August 1999. Interview by the author, Maplewood, MN.
Hillsman, Bill. CEO of North Woods Advertising and Ventura campaign political and media consultant. 26 August 1999. Interview by the author, Minneapolis, MN.
Huddle, Mavis. Ventura campaign secretary. 28 July 1999. Telephone interview by the author, Cambridge, MA, to Northfield, MN.

Humphrey, Hubert H., III. DFL nominee for governor and former Attorney General of Minnesota. 12 August 1999. Interview by the author, Bloomington, MN.

Landy, Mike. Reform Party activist. 16 August 1999. Telephone interview by the author, Mahtomedi, MN, to St. Cloud, MN.

Leary, D. J. Former Vice-President Humphrey aide and longtime Minnesota political observer. 11 September 1999. Interview by the author, St. Paul, MN.

Madsen, Phil. Ventura campaign webmaster. 2 September 1999. Interview by the author, St. Paul, MN.

McCluhan, Rick. Chairman of the Minnesota Reform Party. 24 July 1999. Telephone interview by the author, Cambridge, MA, to Mankato, MN.

McEvoy, Mary. Former Associate Chair of the DFL and Freeman campaign outreach director. 22 July 1999. Telephone interview by the author, Cambridge, MA, to Minneapolis, MN.

Meeks, Jack. Republican National Committeeman from Minnesota. 17 August 1999. Telephone interview by the author, Mahtomedi, MN, to St. Paul, MN.

Mondale, Ted. DFL candidate for governor and current Chair of the Metropolitan Council. 30 August 1999. Interview by the author, St. Paul, MN.

Olsten, Jann. Coleman campaign adviser. 25 August 1999. Telephone interview by the author, Cambridge, MA, to St. Paul, MN.

Senese, Dick. Former DFL Chair. 28 July 1999. Telephone interview by the author, Cambridge, MA, to Northfield, MN.

Shilepsky, Alan. Reform Party candidate for Minnesota Secretary of State. 15 August 1999. Telephone interview by the author, Mahtomedi, MN, to Minneapolis, MN.

Skoglund, Randy. Republican Party official and Coleman campaign worker. 18 August 1999. Telephone interview by the author, Mahtomedi, MN, to Minneapolis, MN.

Sternberg, Bob von. Reporter for the Minneapolis *Star-Tribune* newspaper. 18 July 1999. Telephone interview by the author, Cambridge, MA, to Minneapolis, MN.

Ventura, Governor Jesse. 6 October 1999. Interview by the author, Cambridge, MA.

Maps

State of Minnesota Legislative Coordinating Commission, Geographic Information Systems Office. 1999. "Minnesota Gubernatorial Election Results Based on 1998 Precinct Totals." Published poster. Available from the Geographic Information Systems Office.

Government Documents and Publications

Federal Election Commission. "Frequently Asked Questions About Voter Registration and Voting." Available on the Internet at http://www.fec.gov/pages/faqs.htm.

National Personnel Records Center. Service Record of James George Janos. St. Louis, MO.

————. Enlisted Performance Record of James George Janos. St. Louis, MO.

State of Minnesota Campaign Finance and Public Disclosure Board. 1999. *1998 Campaign Finance Summary*. St. Paul: Offices of the Campaign Finance and Public Disclosure Board.

————. 1999. "Minnesota's Public Subsidy Program." Published memorandum. Available from the author.

State of Minnesota Economic Resource Group. 1998. *1998 Economic Report to the Governor*. St. Paul: Offices of the Economic Resource Group.

State of Minnesota Secretary of State, Elections Division. 1995. *Minnesota Legislative Manual*. 1995–1996 ed. St. Paul: Offices of the Election Division, Secretary of State.

————. 1999. *Minnesota Election Result 1998: State Primary Election and State General Election*. St. Paul: Offices of the Election Division, Secretary of State.

State of Minnesota Planning Agency, Criminal Justice Center. May 1999. *Judging by the Data: Offenders in Minnesota's Juvenile Courts*. St. Paul: Minnesota Planning Agency. Available on the Internet at http://www.mnplan.state.mn.us/cj/index.html.

————. May 1999. *Minnesota Homicides 1985–1997*. St. Paul: Minnesota Planning Agency. Available on the Internet at http://www.mnplan.state.mn.us/cj/index.html.

————. May 1999. *Reported Crimes 1985–1997*. St. Paul: Minnesota Planning Agency. Available on the Internet at http://www.mnplan.state.mn.us/cj/index.html.

————. November 1996. *1996 Children's Services Report Card*. St. Paul: Minnesota Planning Agency. Available on the Internet at http://www.mnplan.state.mn.us/pubs/pub_child.html.

U.S. Department of Commerce. U.S. Census Bureau. 1998. *1998 Statistical Abstract of the United States*. Washington: U.S. Census Bureau. Available on the Internet at http://www.census.gov/prod/www/statistical-abstract-us.html.

Polling Data

Market Strategies, Inc. 1998. *1998 Minnesota Public and Private Polls (Governor's Race)*. Unpublished tracking polling obtained from Chris Georgacas. Includes eight polls conducted by Market Strategies, one poll conducted by Senator Rods Grams polling organization (Tarrance), the four polls published in the *Pioneer Press*, and the five polls published in the *Star-Tribune*. Chatsworth, CA: Market Strategies.

Data Sets

State of Minnesota Secretary of State. *Minnesota Election Results 1998: State Primary Election and State General Election*. Election Division. Computer-readable data file and codebook.

Voter News Service. 1990. *1990 Minnesota General Election Exit Poll.* The Roper Center for Public Opinion Research at the University of Connecticut. Computer-readable data file and codebook.

———. 1994. *1994 Minnesota General Election Exit Poll.* The Roper Center for Public Opinion Research at the University of Connecticut. Computer-readable data file and codebook.

———. 1998. *1998 Minnesota General Election Exit Poll.* The Roper Center for Public Opinion Research at the University of Connecticut. Computer-readable data file and codebook.

Nongovernment Documents

Market Strategies, Inc. 1998. *Minnesota Campaign Update.* Memorandum to Coleman campaign staff of October 28. Obtained from Chris Georgacas, Coleman campaign manager. Chatsworth, CA: Market Strategies.

———. 1998. *Minnesota Issue Agenda.* Graph of percent of respondents calling an issue the first or second most important priority for state government (education, taxes, crime, state spending, family farm, moral values). Obtained from Chris Georgacas, Coleman campaign manager. Chatsworth, CA: Market Strategies.

Videos

Hillsman, Bill. 1998. "Drive to Victory." Written, produced, and directed by Bill Hillsman. 30 seconds. North Woods Advertising, Minneapolis. Loaned to the author from 2 October 1999 until 11 November 1999. Videocassette.

———. 1998. "Jesse Action Figure." Written, produced, and directed by Bill Hillsman. 30 seconds. North Woods Advertising, Minneapolis. Loaned to the author from 2 October 1999 until 11 November 1999. Videocassette.

———. 1998. "Reform Party Ad." Written, produced, and directed by Bill Hillsman. 30 seconds. North Woods Advertising, Minneapolis. Loaned to the author from 2 October 1999 until 11 November 1999. Videocassette.

———. 1998. "Thinker." Written, produced, and directed by Bill Hillsman. 30 seconds. North Woods Advertising, Minneapolis. Loaned to the author from 2 October 1999 until 11 November 1999. Videocassette.

Kiefer, Corey. 1999. "Citizen Jesse." Produced by Red, White, and Blue Brand Productions. Officially licensed merchandise of Ventura for Minnesota, Inc. Purchased by the author. Videocassette.

KSTP-TV. 10 September 1998. "Doug Johnson Profile." Videocassette of newscast given to author by KSTP-TV (ABC affiliate) in Minneapolis. Videocassette.

———. 11 September 1998. "Mark Dayton Profile." Videocassette of newscast given to author by KSTP-TV in Minneapolis. Videocassette.

———. 13 September 1998. "Jesse Ventura Profile." Videocassette of newscast given to author by KSTP-TV in Minneapolis. Videocassette.

———. 1 October 1998. "Brainerd Debate." Video recording of the debate in Brainerd. Given to the author by KSTP-TV in Minneapolis. Videocassette.

————. 31 October 1998. "Last Minute Campaigning." Videocassette of newscast given to author by KSTP-TV in Minneapolis. Videocassette.

————. 4 November 1998. "How We Got Here." Videocassette of newscast given to author by KSTP-TV in Minneapolis. Videocassette.

KTCA-TV. 1998. "October 2nd Debate." Video recording of the October 2 debate sponsored by KTCA-TV. RealVideo. Available on the Internet at http://www.ktca.org/election98/debates.html.

————. 1998. "October 24th Debate." Video recording of the October 24 debate sponsored by KTCA-TV. RealVideo. Available on the Internet at http://www.ktca.org/election98/debates.html.

————. 1998. "October 30th Debate." Video recording of the October 30 debate sponsored by KTCA-TV. RealVideo. Available on the Internet at http://www.ktca.org/election98/debates.html.

League of Women Voters. 1998. "Blake Debate." Video recording of the October 27 debate sponsored by the League of Women Voters. Loaned to the author from the League of Women Voters from 14 January until 13 March 2000. Videocassette.

Minnesota Reform Party. 1999. "We Shocked the World." Purchased from the Minnesota Reform Party. Videocassette.

Newspaper Articles

Many of the articles cited were used in writing the history of the 1998 gubernatorial campaign. For this reason, the following articles from the Minneapolis *Star Tribune* and the *St. Paul Pioneer Press* are ordered chronologically.

Minneapolis *Star Tribune*

18 November 1994. Dane Smith. "The 'L' Word." Minneapolis *Star Tribune,* p. 22A.

5 November 1997. Doug Grow. "Coleman's Next Step: Candidacy for Governor?" Minneapolis *Star Tribune,* p. 2B.

6 November 1997. Dane Smith and Kevin Duschshere. "Republicans Announce Plans to Draft Coleman." Minneapolis *Star Tribune,* p. 1A.

27 January 1998. Dane Smith. "Ventura Joins the Fray Race to Follow Carlson." Minneapolis *Star Tribune,* p. 1B.

3 February 1998. Dane Smith. "In the Gubernatorial Fund-raising Race, Dayton, Benson Lead Crowded Packs." Minneapolis *Star Tribune,* p. 1A.

16 February 1998. Dane Smith. "It's Official: Coleman Joins the Crowd." Minneapolis *Star Tribune,* p. 1B.

25 February 1998. Dennis J. McGrath. "State Sen. Terwilliger Leaves GOP Gubernatorial Race." Minneapolis *Star Tribune,* p. 2B.

1 March 1998. Dennis J. McGrath. "Coleman, Humphrey Off to Quick Starts." Minneapolis *Star Tribune,* p. 1A.

23 March 1998. Robert Whereatt, Dane Smith, and Conrad deFiebre. "Inside Talk." Minneapolis *Star Tribune,* p. 3B.

4 June 1998. Robert Whereatt, Dane Smith, and Conrad deFiebre. "Humphrey Leads Pack." Minneapolis *Star Tribune*, p. 1A.

26 July 1998. "By the Way . . . " Minneapolis *Star Tribune*, p. 5B.

27 July 1998. "Candidate Quiz." Minneapolis *Star Tribune*, p. 3B.

14 August 1998. Dane Smith. "Coleman Under Fire for Gun Position." Minneapolis *Star Tribune*, p. 1A.

18 September 1998. Patricia Lopez-Baden. "Coleman Details Tax-Cut Proposal." Minneapolis *Star Tribune*, p. 1B.

20 September 1998. "The November Lineup." Minneapolis *Star Tribune*, p. 4A.

22 September 1998. "Ventura Pushes for Smaller Classes in Elementary School." Minneapolis *Star Tribune*, p. 3B.

23 September 1998. Robert Whereatt. "Poll Indicates Humphrey Has Strong Lead over Coleman." Minneapolis *Star Tribune*, p. 1A.

26 September 1998. Patricia Lopez-Baden. "Ad Watch: Campaign '98." Minneapolis *Star Tribune*, p. 3B.

5 October 1998. AP Wire Service. "Gubernatorial Candidates Oppose Mandatory Helmets for Motorcyclists." Minneapolis *Star Tribune*.

7 October 1998. Dane Smith. "Campaign Becomes a Numbers Game." Minneapolis *Star Tribune*, p. 4B.

10 October 1998. Bill Wareham. "Coleman Says Humphrey Ads Lied About His Farm Comments." AP Wire Service, Dateline: St. Paul.

10 October 1998. Patricia Lopez-Baden. "Coleman Files Complaint Against DFL." Minneapolis *Star Tribune*, p. 1B.

12 October 1998. Robert Whereatt. "DFL Sen. Bob Lessard Backs Coleman." Minneapolis *Star Tribune*, p. 5B.

17 October 1998. Bill Cooper. "Humphrey Shares Blame for State's Increase in Crime." Minneapolis *Star Tribune*, p. 23A.

20 October 1998. Robert Whereatt. "Suddenly, It's a Dead Heat." Minneapolis *Star Tribune*, p. 1A.

21 October 1998. Conrad de Fiebre, Bob von Sternberg, and Dane Smith. "Shift in Poll Creates Some Political Ripple." Minneapolis *Star Tribune*, p. 1B.

24 October 1998. Patricia Lopez-Baden. "Candidates Trade Volleys in Dispute on Gay Marriage." Minneapolis *Star Tribune*, p. 1B.

25 October 1998. Dane Smith. "Candidates Do Very Little Debating." Minneapolis *Star Tribune*, p. 1B.

25 October 1998. "Star Tribune Endorsements." Minneapolis *Star Tribune*, p. 24A.

25 October 1998. Dane Smith. "Norm Coleman." Minneapolis *Star Tribune*, p. 14A.

25 October 1998. Robert Whereatt. "Hubert Humphrey III." Minneapolis *Star Tribune*, 15A.

30 October 1998. Patrick Sweeney and Jim Ragsdale. "Governor Candidates Fan Out to Light Fire Under Faithful." Minneapolis *Star Tribune*, p. 1A.

4 November 1998. Dane Smith and Robert Whereatt. "VENTURA WINS." Minneapolis *Star Tribune*, p. 1A.

15 August 1999. Dane Smith. "Marching to Its Own Drummers." Minneapolis *Star Tribune* Sunday Edition, pp. 10A–11A.

St. Paul Pioneer Press

27 August 1998. Steven Dornfield. "Humphrey: An Old-fashioned Liberal Who Believes in Government." *St. Paul Pioneer Press,* p. 16A.

3 September 1998. "How in Touch with Real Life Are the Candidates for the State's Highest Office? We Asked Them Some Everyday Questions, and Here's What They Had to Say." *St. Paul Pioneer Press* Special Section, "Your Primary Choice Voter's Guide," p. 9M.

4 September 1998. Jim Ragsdale. "Political Candidates Eagerly Weigh In on Strike." *St. Paul Pioneer Press,* p. 1A.

8 September 1998. Jim Ragsdale. "Contenders Labor for Votes Across State." *St. Paul Pioneer Press,* p. 1C.

13 September 1998. Jack Coffman. "Getting on the DFL Bus." *St. Paul Pioneer Press,* p. 1C.

16 September 1998. Patrick Sweeney. "Primary Is About Meeting Citizen's Role, Many Say." *St. Paul Pioneer Press,* p. 1A.

16 September 1998. Patrick Sweeney. "Coleman: After an Easy Primary Season, GOP Nominee Has to Get Down to Business." *St. Paul Pioneer Press,* p. 8A.

17 September 1998. Jack B. Coffman. "On Their Mark, Get Set, Go." *St. Paul Pioneer Press,* p. 1A.

17 September 1998. Jim Ragsdale. "On Their Mark, Get Set, Go." *St. Paul Pioneer Press,* p. 1A.

17 September 1998. "Minnesota Race for Governor: Details, Stark Contrasts Might Lure Voters Back." *St. Paul Pioneer Press,* p. 12A.

18 September 1998. Tom Powers. "Election May Hinge on Stadium Issue." *St. Paul Pioneer Press,* p. 1C.

19 September 1998. Jim Ragsdale. "Humphrey Says Debates Must Include Ventura." *St. Paul Pioneer Press,* p. 1A.

20 September 1998. Dave Beal. "Business Fears Humphrey Victory." *St. Paul Pioneer Press,* p. 1D.

20 September 1998. Jim Ragsdale. "And the Winners Are . . ." *St. Paul Pioneer Press,* p. 3C.

23 September 1998. Jim Ragsdale. "GOP Lashed for Running Ads After Brown Death." *St. Paul Pioneer Press,* p. 1B.

24 September 1998. Thomas J. Collins. "Humphrey, Coleman Wary of 'Everyman' Ventura." *St. Paul Pioneer Press,* p. 1A.

25 September 1998. Nick Coleman. "Mourners Remember Minnesota's 'Wonderful Lady.'" *St. Paul Pioneer Press,* p. 1A.

28 September 1998. Jack B. Coffman. "Coleman, Humphrey Exchange Accusations." *St. Paul Pioneer Press,* p. 1E.

29 September 1998. Jack B. Coffman. "Carlson Stumps on Behalf of Coleman." *St. Paul Pioneer Press,* p. 3C.

1 October 1998. Carl Cummins. "Two Negatives May Equal Positive for Ventura." *St. Paul Pioneer Press,* p. 17A.

2 October 1998. Jim Ragsdale. "Classic Tax Fight Takes Shape in Campaign." *St. Paul Pioneer Press,* p. 1A.

7 October 1998. Patrick Sweeney. "Iron Range Hears Ventura's Siren Song in Debate." *St. Paul Pioneer Press,* p. 13A.

9 October 1998. "Barkley: Ventura Campaign Has Dire Cash Woes." *St. Paul Pioneer Press,* p. 7C.

15 October 1998. Jim Ragsdale. "Poll: Humphrey Tops, Schools Key Issue." *St. Paul Pioneer Press,* p. 1A.

18 October 1998. "Our Choice for Governor: Coleman Will Lead Us to a Brighter Future." *St. Paul Pioneer Press,* p. 16A.

18 October 1998. Nick Coleman. "What Does KQ's Success Say About Us?" *St. Paul Pioneer Press,* p. 1B.

20 October 1998. Jim Ragsdale. "Humphrey Wants Special Session on Tax Relief for Farmers." *St. Paul Pioneer Press,* p. 2B.

22 October 1998. Patrick Sweeney. "Ventura: Consider Legalizing Prostitution." *St. Paul Pioneer Press,* p. 1A.

23 October 1998. Patrick Sweeney. "Ventura Wrestles with Prostitution Question." *St. Paul Pioneer Press,* p. 1B.

26 October 1998. Nick Coleman. "Ventura's Straight Talk Merits Respect." *St. Paul Pioneer Press,* p. 1C.

27 October 1998. Jim Ragsdale. "Campaign 1998 Minnesota." *St. Paul Pioneer Press,* p. 2C.

28 October 1998. Jim Ragsdale. "Interest Groups Roll Out Last-Minute Election Ads." *St. Paul Pioneer Press,* p. 4C.

28 October 1998. Joe Soucheray. "The, uh, Mind Keeps Up His Fearless Charge." *St. Paul Pioneer Press,* p. 1C.

29 October 1998. "The Jesse Ventura Effect." *St. Paul Pioneer Press,* p. 14A.

29 October 1998. Jack B. Coffman. "Candidates Cordial as Campaigns Crisscross." *St. Paul Pioneer Press,* p. 1A.

1 November 1998. Jim Ragsdale and Patrick Sweeney. "Campaign Reaches Peak." *St. Paul Pioneer Press,* p. 1A.

1 November 1998. D. J. Tice. "Great Governors." *St. Paul Pioneer Press,* p. 1G.

25 July 1999. Russell Fridley. "Minnesota Has a Long History of Tripartisanship." *St. Paul Pioneer Press* Sunday Edition, p. 16A.

Non–Twin Cities Newspapers

Higgins, A. Jay. 9 November 1994. "Snowe, Baldacci Claim Victory; King-Brennan Race a Tossup." *Bangor Daily News,* p. 1A.

Wohlforth, Charles. 25 November 1990. "Hickel's Victory Came on 'Wild Card' Vote." *Anchorage Daily News,* p. A1.

INDEX

ABOUT THE BOOK

Many commentators and political scientists have dismissed Jesse Ventura's election as governor of Minnesota as a fluke of celebrity. In this account of Ventura's campaign to victory, Jacob Lentz shows that it was instead Minnesota's unique electoral rules, coupled with on-target campaign dynamics, that enabled a third-party candidate to reach high office.

This first complete account of Ventura's victory draws on tantalizing details from the race to show that campaigns definitely do matter. Interviews with key players, exit polls, analyses of media coverage, and assessments of advertisements and debate performance also contribute to a compelling case study of U.S. politics at the state and local level.

Moving beyond old theories about structural barriers to fringe candidates, *Electing Jesse Ventura* makes abundantly clear that third-party candidates can seize the favor of the U.S. electorate—and actually benefit from their lack of ties to the major parties—by emphasizing their pragmatism and independence.

Jacob Lentz, a native Minnesotan, is a scholar of political science and a graduate of Harvard University.